HOW TO Fire YOUR HUSBAND IN easy STEPS

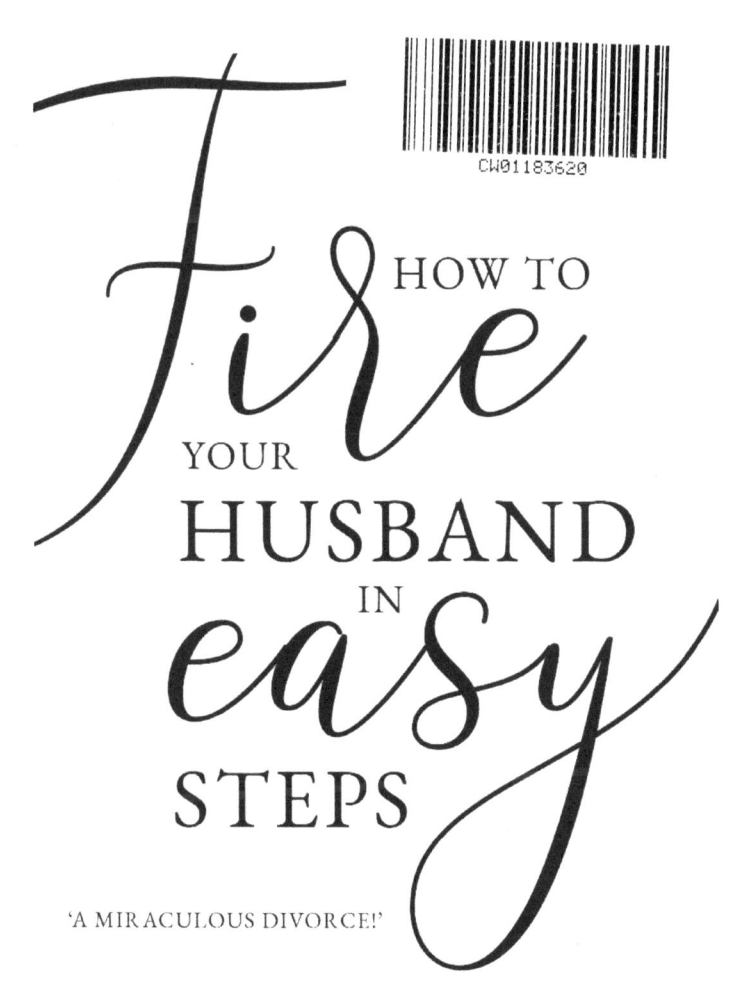

'A MIRACULOUS DIVORCE!'

CHRISTEL HOLST-SANDE COWDREY

CRANTHORPE
MILLNER

Copyright © Christel Holst-Sande Cowdrey (2023)

The right of Christel Holst-Sande Cowdrey to be identified as author of this work has been asserted by her in accordance with section 77 and 78 of the Copyright, Designs and Patents Act 1988.

All rights reserved. No part of this publication may be reproduced, stored in a retrieval system, or transmitted in any form or by any means, electronic, mechanical, photocopying, recording, or otherwise, without the prior permission of the publishers.

Any person who commits any unauthorised act in relation to this publication may be liable to criminal prosecution and civil claims for damages.

First published by Cranthorpe Millner Publishers (2023)

ISBN 978-1-80378-079-5 (Paperback)

www.cranthorpemillner.com

Cranthorpe Millner Publishers

'A brave and compelling account of Christel's journey through an emotional maelstrom of blessings and betrayals. These are life experiences that all lives can learn from, deeply emotional and at the same time hugely empowering.' – Claire Philpott

'This is a raw account of a woman moving on from the breakdown of her marriage, abandoning bitterness and recriminations and refusing to apportion blame to any one party. Christel is an accredited mediator and is thus able to look at the end of her marriage objectively, whilst setting out her philosophy for a happier parting of ways. Having seen her own parents' marriage deteriorate and the repercussions on the children of that family, Christel was determined to take another path, which is sensitively and intelligently dealt with by drawing on her own experiences as a daughter, sister, wife and mother.' – Fiona Criswell

'As a member of Christel's family, I found much of her heartache difficult to read, but I realised that the challenges she faced were written in love. In facing those obstacles and letting them go, every new step revealed a lesson. I believe each one shared here may be valuable to us all and each step is beautifully expressed.' – Charlotte Sande-Vine

'Christel's forensic account of relationships and events that formed navigation points in the journey her life is compelling. This story is more than soulful and thought provoking, it is healing – a balm for the stings of life and a wake-up call for all, no matter their part in the theatre of life. Christel's message is one of responsibility for self-awareness and development of our unconscious 'being' and its impacts and outcomes. Only then can we fully account for ourselves as human beings.' – Lorna McDowell

In Gratitude

Without suffering or admissions of my failures I would never have been inspired to write this book. I am certain, I may never have completed it.
There are parts that feel uncomfortable, they have the power to dissolve my resolve momentarily, but then that's fair enough.

I add with a wry smile that I thank my former husband for one hell of a road trip. I thank my sons for their endurance, because we have all learned that truth is the only way to live, that a smoother journey is possible when we summon strength just when our burdens may feel insurmountable – then, that is when we find we are living in Grace.

– Christel

Foreword
by Julius Lindahl Cowdrey

Throughout my childhood, until my late teens, I was fortunate to have a strong, loving, fun and stable foundation – an unbroken home. And then one evening, my mother sat by me, I recall I was playing the piano at the time, and she said she felt she must divorce my father, for adultery.

The confusion and shock were something I had never experienced before. I had thought marriage was forever. My father had been my hero. I thought they were fine! In that second, I changed. I grew up; felt I became a man. I felt vulnerable but found strength I hadn't known I had, to be there for my mother. But through her sadness she was so calm, so kind and said nothing, not a word against him – but how?

I threw every expletive I could muster about him; she would listen and simply say, "He loves you; you mean the world to him, you are the best thing in our lives, he is a devoted father."

My mother didn't want us having a negative view of him. I was silently so frustrated by her, angry even.

It took me a while to understand her maturity, her innate strength and her grace. She made me see that if people hurt us, it reflects their state of mind. My father's adultery wasn't anything to do with my mother; it wasn't a measure of his love for his family.

After years of resentment towards him, Fabian and I decided to forgive him too. My mother wanted that for us.

It is because of her that I have a relationship with my dad, a very good one. It's because of her that I have a deep respect for women; a strong empathy and rationale; an ability to listen and begin to understand people's actions. I feel very lucky.

I know this book will help many to find the strength to

divorce in a calm, mature and empathic way… and most importantly, the right way. Then they will also survive to build a new and fulfilling life.

With love,

Julius

Foreword
by Fabian Kruuse Cowdrey

Well, may I begin this foreword by expressing how proud I am to call the author of this book my mother.

Since a tragedy ensued behind our family walls, my twin and I have rekindled a special love for our dad. Without the selflessness, forgiveness and unwavering love of our mother, it would have been an impossibility.

I was left dumbfounded by the approach that she adopted during this mindless heartbreak. I can say with conviction that it wasn't her kindness that surprised me, but simply her refusal to accept that anyone, including the love of her life, had a right to ruin her life or the life of her sons.

My mother has defied the odds, curing the poison that was set to run through our family. How? Well, that will soon become 'Christel' clear as you are introduced to the most courageous person I know.

The journey you are about to embark on will introduce you to the power of motherhood, the art of releasing bitterness and the unconquerable power of faith.

The words written in this book are an expression of vulnerability and in that you'll find its power. If you truly allow it, this book will lead you to the closure and peace that you deserve.

With love,

Fabian

Foreword
by Benjamin Quin-Fellows

People describe writing as a vocation of escapism. A setting in which one is able to forget the present day and escape to a destination of their choice. However, within the context of this book, Christel does not write to 'escape', she writes to reflect on situations in her life, bravely confronting difficult scenarios whilst cherishing special moments and relationships.

Seeing these reflections compartmentalised in such a mature and warm manner in this book encourages the reader to mirror the intricate self-analysis Christel exhibits. The intention of this being to help the reader navigate their life's journeys and empower them to take charge of their destination.

The passion I saw in Christel when writing this book is only matched by the passion of its content actualising in reality – her spending time with family, recalling childhood stories with her father. The authenticity of emotion is evident and accessible to all.

My personal reflection on reading this book, and the self-analytical conclusion it leaves me with, is one of gratitude. Gratitude for my past, no matter the subsequent implication. Gratitude for the lessons life has prompted me to learn, and gratitude for the author of this book who has had such a profound impact on my life.

With love,

Ben

Table of Contents

Preface i
Chapter One
    The Driver in Relationships 1
Chapter Two
    The Crisis 5
Chapter Three
    A State of Collapse 9
Chapter Four
    The Truth Will Out & The Veneer Falls 14
Chapter Five
    A Deathly Stupor 18
Chapter Six
    Halfway There 22
Chapter Seven
    The Domino Effect 26
Chapter Eight
    Why the Soul Must Weep 29
Chapter Nine
    Victory or Defeat, Your Choice 35
Chapter Ten

Retain, Never Detain a Soul 39
Chapter Eleven
  Two Masterful Attributes 47
Chapter Twelve
  Forgiveness is the Force Behind Survival 49
Chapter Thirteen
  Hidden Signals of Deceit 53
Chapter Fourteen
  FEAR: False Evidence Appearing Real 56
Chapter Fifteen
  The Allure of My Father 58
Chapter Sixteen
  The Glorious Subterfuge That Is Motherhood 61
Chapter Seventeen
  The Interloper 64
Chapter Eighteen
  Gratitude Magic 69
Chapter Nineteen
  Peace Vanquishes All – One of the Universal Laws 72
Chapter Twenty
  Cheated and the Cheater 75
Chapter Twenty-One
  Precious Friends 78
Chapter Twenty-Two
  Revisiting the Manual 82
Chapter Twenty-Three
  The Fear in a Child 95
Chapter Twenty-Four
  Scripting Our Children 98

Chapter Twenty-Five
Truth: The Abundant Blitz of Consequence 104

Chapter Twenty-Six
My Debut in Court 110

Chapter Twenty-Seven
A Daughter's Turn 115

Chapter Twenty-Eight
Evidence of Disease Profiles and Paradigms 122

Chapter Twenty-Nine
Life's 'Coaches' 126

Chapter Thirty
Unconscious vs Conscious Parenting 128

Chapter Thirty-One
Sabotaged – Triggers As Anchors 133

Chapter Thirty-Two
'Do or Die' – The Hyperbolic Expressive 137

Chapter Thirty-Three
Don't Look Back 139

Chapter Thirty-Four
Earliest Instructions 144

Chapter Thirty-Five
Lessons From My Grandparents 147

Chapter Thirty-Six
A Privilege to Walk the Whole Way to the Gate 153

Chapter Thirty-Seven
Lemon-Lipped Women 159

Chapter Thirty-Eight
Save Our Souls 161

Epilogue 166

Preface

I recall a time I once absentmindedly remarked to a friend: "There may not be a faithful man in the whole-wide world." He slammed his tightened fist on the table and blurted, "I should bloody well hope there is!". With that, I felt something… I think it was hope. In that moment, a burden may even have been lifted.

I have been told off often, for reaching for a mitigating circumstance when it comes to duplicitous partners, for suggesting that perhaps their intention was never to hurt anyone at all. Perhaps their partner was being less attentive, perhaps their attention was focused elsewhere: children, pets, work, looking after Granny – you get my drift.

Honestly, and in keeping one's own counsel of course, I am positive I was nowhere near his mind when the luscious force of lust swept over him. No, I was far, far away!

Whilst I sought to take my part in the responsibility

of this uncoupling, I could never reconcile that anyone should carry the responsibility of a partner's head on the pillow, or a body infused with another's. In a compatible and easy marriage, is anyone prepared to suffer and wake up to a partner whose burgeoning ardour is elsewhere and accept it? Is one able simply to 'turn the other cheek', or whatever Jackie O may have said, when asked what she would do if she suspected infidelity?

I received an inner voice of intervention, it urged: "Let it go! But how and why should I?" I asked. "Just… try…" was levied at me and with that the voice sank to a sepulchral tone saying, "Either that or face a seeping darkness, pulsating through you demonic, for a lifetime."

And so, I did. I let go.

Here are my considerations: letting go was for my health and my life's sake. I needed to survive with sanity on point.

I have been told that the title I chose for this book could be mistakenly perceived as a story of one-upmanship and a disparaging of the other. I was urged to change it. But this title was never intended to claim superiority or belittle another but rather, in using this title, I hoped for the chance to share a smile through what is indeed a grim phase for any one of us, going through such disarray as divorce.

It came about when I was away on a training course in Canada surrounded by a hundred or more students and we began to introduce ourselves. I listened intently and when it got around to me, I was asked, "How about you Christel? Husband, children?"

It came to me in a flash! I hadn't relinquished my marriage. I had sacrificed much for it – all quite natural and nothing new. The truth is, I felt saddened beyond expression but felt much was at stake.

My own father had been unfaithful and his father before him. When I did reflect, many years after the initial crushing of my trusting and devoted heart, I accepted that I was, in some unexpressed paradigm within my psyche, complicit.

Had I assumed that men such as my grandfather, father, father-in-law and husband, who all shared the same exquisite sensibilities of gentleness, kindness and respect were, despite these traits of a good man, incapable of fidelity? Was it fair of me to assume that most men were incapable of singular devotion, so that most of their wives were to suffer and wake up to their partner's rousing ardour flitting in and out of a good marriage?

None of the men I have spoken with for this book had ever intended to hurt their wives. They compartmentalised thoughts of their partner when away on business trips and found the allure of 'out of sight out of mind' irresistible, irrepressible.

No blame was ever levied on their spouse.

Sex with another didn't affect their deep love for

their partner and commitment to the family. "Absolutely not!" was the retort from every single man I asked!

If it came to light, as it did for some, they seemed to redeem themselves, because their wives deduced (as I had) that they had a lot 'on deposit'. I asked whether a blindness to their weakness for available women was perhaps forgiven by their wives, in favour of the bigger picture?

The reply was "it would seem so". Forgiveness by their wives was done for life's sake, stability's sake, the children's sake, friendship and allegiance's sake and for the sake of sharing one another's burdens.

Whatever it was, it was for another's sake. Most men did finally concede that it was for their own sakes too.

I had been extremely close to my father. I adored my father-in-law. I had spoken to them of unfaithfulness many times. My father-in-law had what he called a fragile heart.

I asked if his heart was heavy? He said, "Yes. I have left broken hearts in my wake and I cannot change that, but that was never my intention. Never. Do you believe me?"

I believed him utterly!

My father was similar; kind and gentle to a fault on many an occasion, less contrite perhaps, when women fell at his feet. When I witnessed it, as his daughter, I found those women embarrassing. He was a more handsome version of that old accomplished and handsome actor of his time, George Peppard. I would dine with him and girlfriends would exclaim how handsome my companion at dinner was! They simply never believed it was my (young) father; he was twenty-three when I was born. He was flirty and funny; he loved the attention. Did that therefore render him incapable of beckoning in forgiveness, the way he carelessly reeled in women?

With that understanding, I was always able to casually remark with a smile, "Well, my husband was here for some twenty-five years, but he had to be fired for his misdemeanours." That line caused such spontaneous laughter and in doing so, swiftly deflected any awkward questions and allowed me to maintain my dignity. Everyone has an opinion and with that in mind, I have learned that a loose tongue and sharp response hold no trump card.

Heartache is an all too frequent malaise, best managed with a sane mind, infused with sound sleep. Despite the anger, incredulity and shock – it can be done. With need for survival as the latest bedfellow, these components serve as a dam to control the level of any bitterness that seeks to overwhelm.

'Persistence is to the character of man as carbon is to steel.' – Napoleon Hill

There is truly no better way. Decisions must be made

and managed with support and it is to this end (with hopefully some humour) that I would like to share my thinking and maybe even inspire you to move forward, by firing your husband in easy steps.

*

I don't really know whether my personal path, in prepping me for the inevitable disaster of casting out my marriage, was prolonged through patience or empathy. I had full understanding of my former husband, knowing his own heartache of the same nature was experienced at the exact same age as that of our two sons; I suspect there are no coincidences when it comes to any of our family's disposition regarding such memories.

There is strong evidence that no disease is categorically inherited, but rather it is the *disposition* to that disease that sits in the subconscious mind as a 'given'. Not if, but when. These inherited feelings, by way of memory, are passed down in fear, often hidden from the conscious mind by the bearer.

Perhaps in keeping it hidden deep inside the bowels of my being, it was a weakness I displayed as strength, one I justified, in order to keep the four of us together. I had to save them from the imminent danger; I couldn't chop my family into a million pieces in one fell swoop. I would persevere to save them from that greater danger.

It's a tricky one and I didn't fully comprehend how slow, but sure, my grieving was. Friends have continually and very sweetly marvelled at my so-called dignity.

For me, I promise this has not been conscious action and is a natural part of my integral system. I didn't have to *try* to be dignified. If I could have expressed anger, humiliation, disdain even, then I'm sure I would have. It may be generational inheritance and may possibly have been healthier to erupt like a volcano, but I'm not convinced – hence the book.

I find outbursts of anger quite hideous, self-centred and a deafness to the truth. For me, coming unstrung and blaming the other is weakness. But when the chips are down, I am at my most raw and strong. Survival kicks in. I clamber aboard my 'steely raft' that will see me through such tumultuous waters… anyway, a life spent in prison for murder sits uncomfortably with me…

I joke, of course!

I have a psychiatrist friend who says that cultures respond differently to extremities. He knows the Swedes collectively experienced a metamorphosis, that expresses itself as a reaction seeking resolution (post the Viking bludgeoning experiences), that runs through the individuals, as blood coursed through their veins during Viking combat in days gone by. I am assured cultural studies determine this as a proven theory and I do respect that – there is obvious logic in this too.

He said, "Such cultures as the Zulus settle in blood." In the West, hopefully, we still aspire to find a way to meet on the bridge, seeking resolution.

My former best friend and husband is the chosen father of my children. Women have an abiding instinct in identifying 'the chosen one'. We stood at the altar, our vows booming through us as we listened intently to the vicar with every cell of our beings. The wherewithal to somehow forget those powerful messages when lying in bed with another lover is a magnitude, considering the vows we made. They felt as though they were spoken directly to God, since we gave our promises to Him, as well as to one another.

I wonder, does the absence of a church marriage dissipate the seriousness and steadfastness for which we subordinate our personal ambitions to unify with another?

Can marrying on a beach, or on a Las Vegas film set, or in our home, potentially make the ceremony less dictatorial, or conversely, could it perhaps make it more empowering? Is it not intended to be a sobering moment of commitment? It may dissipate the approach, perhaps a more modern one to the union but still, marriage is most definitely a contract.

A contract with one's higher nature and ultimately, a contract of loyalty towards our spouse: 'until death do us part'. There are those with a deeply ingrained sense of morality and experience of longevity in marriage, whose families have been successful in this regard, who may find this paradigm a powerhouse for them. Would they cheat, or are they probably less likely to?

What keeps them there? Maybe it's the security of being supported by a family network where marriage has remained sacrosanct over many generations. It may be a sense of sure commitment to the other and a determined and deliberately blinkered view of the overwhelming availability of other men and other women or, to those who are having fun and deeming themselves not responsible for their partner's happiness, it may simply be the commitment to their spouse.

We are all put together with the spoon-fed views of our parents – those and the pointers from our innermost circles contributing and dictating how we mature.

Whether these paradigms sabotage our personal success or celebrate and create it are debatable, but all are still highly possible and valuable considerations.

There is a lot of evidence in the power of relinquishing those predetermined thoughts, should we wish to explore this as a way of further developing our paths.

*

Whenever I enter a seminar, listen to a podcast, read a book, begin to write an article or prepare a talk, I focus on how I feel most touched or impacted by others when they speak to me. There are a zillion self-help books and courses to attend, fun workshops to learn new skills and interviews with psychologists and doctors qualified to manage and instruct those who are struggling with a disease. I have tremendous respect for all of them.

Because I feel so impacted by the support and understanding of others going through what might have felt like my own impending disasters, I began to understand how I personally listen and learn best in my own life. Any response I may have will always have a ricocheting effect on those in my immediate sphere, particularly my sons. To not give this consideration would have spelled disaster for their balanced approach to crises in their own lives – on the basis that we do as our parents do, rather than do as they say – and it also matters wholeheartedly to me that I put myself second in consideration of their happiness.

I'm sad to say that most of us, whilst justified, will react to a crisis without due caution as to its impact on those around us. Many say to me, "Who cares? I can't live for others well-being." But yes, you can and, although I hate the word 'should'… we all should.

When the very foundations of my life felt like an earthquake beneath my feet, threatening to cast me aside, they pushed me to the point of questioning what all this was for if I was so unimportant, so worthless and loved so little. I heard a voice, asking me gently to step aside from this nonsensical thinking, to wake up and quietly move away from the line of fire.

This idea that everything was my fault was untrue. I realised that it was up to me to stay very quiet, rather than get down in the dirt and fight. I felt that if my path was changing, or the path around me, I was to be vigilant and alert and consider the decisions of others.

I was not to be my own worst enemy by digging in my heels. Frankly to be driven by something projected onto me, without stopping for a second to recognise another person's desire for change, their desire for a new path, would simply prolong the combat. I thought about my family and the train that had steamed through my husband's parents' marriage and my own parents' marriage. I considered that unless I stopped being a passenger on the train, this generational drive would not only impact me in my behaviour and family relationships, but also our children's future, their relationships and potentially their marriages and the scripting of their own children. Much is known about scripting children, it's not new and it's not sensationalist – it is a responsibility and it is sound advice to consider all actions as a parent: our children must come first. I thought about the innocent child I had been when I'd observed disloyalty between my parents and the incessant pain it caused my mother and my father. I had shared the memories of similar heartache in my husband's family that had been endured during similar challenges.

I had not been foolish in marrying my children's father. I had made the biggest decision in my life to share my heart, soul and sinew for a successful marriage, one full of fun, teamwork and play and the joy of our children. The break-up tore me apart as any end of a relationship tears everyone's life apart. I'm not alone. It tore away at my everyday world, my responsibilities, the division of labour and our security. The camaraderie and conversations we would have for hours on end were silenced. It was definitely a lonesome space to inhabit.

When I was asked to write about it, I trembled within. The title had been a flippant deterrent to gossip. I didn't want to hurt anyone at all with my thoughts. I explained the purpose to my sons and closest friends who told me to be brave and speak up, that I would be writing from love, but I did feel very isolated and leaned a lot on my own understanding until I learned that is never ideal. I started to pray and meditate. My grasp of anything in the future was cast in mottled light.

I just slept when my babies slept and stayed, as much as possible, enveloped in their sunshine rather than facing the questions with a grimace when they asked me, "When is Daddy coming?"

I recall one of the boys asked where he was and I said he was staying in London because of the icy roads. He looked me squarely in the eye, barely three years old and said, "Mummy, they grit the roads you know!" We were visiting a godparent who was sharing the load, the one who is now married to my former husband and is no longer a godparent – role rescinded!

*

When I visit a seminar, I want to be changed. I want my paradigms to be shifted into another hemisphere. I want to be touched and moved by the speaker and for my heart to be awakened, perhaps even broken a little by a truth that I may never have considered before, a chink where new light can get in.

That is the reason I write, for those scudding clouds to be dispersed by the light. All we have is the relationship with ourselves and the experiences that have allied themselves to us and changed our path; some we have trudged through, as though we were walking in treacle or in a sandstorm in a desert without water, all the while feeling a burgeoning sense of collapse before taking another step. There are those alongside us that have taken us higher, lifted our spirits and shown us future possibilities we thought we might never encounter.

They may have sheltered us in our abyss and convinced us that soon, if we keep looking up, we will see that blinding shaft of light, alighting each step to a new place.

We can be finally woken by our inner selves, that part

of us that finds patience when we are incandescent with fury, or the surprise of shedding tears for another person's heartache when they have acknowledged they have brought a disaster upon themselves and courageously asked for forgiveness. Feeling is embedded in every memory and feeling is what makes us feel alive – the secret.

We have all, at some time, felt a presence around us, when at the point of no return we have shaken ourselves from a stupor of fear, reaching out for support and feeling so grateful to have received it.

I wanted to simply say that all I possess is my own experience and it is all I can share. I don't need to teach another soul a thing – we are all marching to the beat of our own drum on our own life path.

My authentic self is all I have. Of course, there is much that is autobiographical here, but it is not intended to be clever or egocentric. If, in sharing my story, another human being like me may find a similar way forward, then writing this memoir has been worthwhile.

The reason there is history of my family in the book is not to bore you, but because I know that generational factors are inevitable reasons for some of our behaviour and my actions. I think you will find the 'inheritance' from your family in you too.

The words spoken to me growing up still resonate with me. I am at the mercy of my father's words: "Find a mitigating circumstance for another person's behaviour – if it hurts you, question yourself and ask, did I do something to cause this? If you did, be quick to ask for forgiveness because a quick 'sorry!' doesn't heal. It takes courage to admit you're wrong. If you are not wrong, turn the other cheek and acknowledge that the opponent is transferring their problem onto you and move along."

I hope the steps throughout this book support you in starting again after what feels like ploughing through disaster. If I can begin a new life with almost miraculous healing and courage to love each day then, trust me, so can you.

I send you my best love,

Christel

Chapter One
The Driver in Relationships

I have great friends whose children are marrying the copy of their parent – sometimes the physical copies! I also have friends who are adopted and, whilst the evidence doesn't implicate happiness depending upon natural or adoptive parents, some have told me they feel there is an element of caution, an anxious, innate fear of abandonment when it comes to commitment.

I believe relationship and partnership in every form is what determines our path, our success in love and as parents, in friendship and in business. However, sometimes, it may still seem preferable to remain alone, rather than settling into an agreement of convenience driven by fear of solitude. It is known we follow predetermined, unconscious paradigms, some generational, that control us subconsciously; that we do as our parents do and not what they say. Sometimes it can be difficult to step away and define ourselves as individuals.

Living with a muddled identity could sometimes be drawn from the absence of the biological mother or father and it wouldn't be surprising if this could lead to parents becoming too liberal or conversely too strict – one as extreme and as chaotic as the other. I feel it helps to unravel our reactions, to be gentle on ourselves and give ourselves some understanding and compassion when we feel vulnerable.

According to psychologists, too tight or too loose a leash in parenting is a misplaced directive and can project pressure onto the child. A child assuming full autonomy is always fearful, since they feel they are the steer in their world, a world they know little of. When we as parents feel we empower our child by handing over the reins, we may unwittingly create in them a level of anxiety. I recall a story of the children playing football without a referee and the arguing and unrest it caused. The referee arrived late, but when he did, he blew his whistle, re-started the match, allowed the children their freedom and fun to play and they had the game of their lives, demonstrating that guidance and direction are worth considering in all things.

Dominance in our parenting is not recommended either, rather a stepping in with guidance and direction – becoming the 'frame around their picture', so to speak, with pride, makes the child feel balanced and supported.

As we are growing up, we do most definitely drink

in the rules and the non-negotiable directives on the road. What would it take to re-direct to our own choices and ambitions?

One step would be to read the book *Self-Image & Psycho-Cybernetics* by Dr Maxwell Maltz, MD FICS Cosmetic Surgeon. I found it fascinating and it alerted me to the power of the subconscious mind and how it governs our thoughts.

Dr Maltz would operate and repair an extremely damaged face and find that despite the regained normality, some patients still felt ugly, vulnerable and unchanged. His study into self-image began. In 1960 he wrote his book on the subject and the science involved.

'Cybernetics' loosely translated from the Greek is 'the helmsman who steers his ship to port', 'to navigate or govern'. Dr Maxwell Maltz uses the term to talk about steering your thoughts towards a productive, useful goal, to reach a peaceful mind.

An easy way to grasp cybernetics would be to consider an aircraft predestined to arrive at its destination automatically; cybernetically, there would be a 'course-correct' if it veered off course.

The teachings of pyscho-cybernetics are timeless because they are based on solid science and provide a prescription for thinking and acting, which leads to quantifiable results.

I would highly recommend Dr Maltz's book as a powerhouse of information that is easily understood and therefore can be implemented with understanding.

When it comes to rejection, we can try to alter what is an automatic response or (another used term) a built-in servomechanism.

The cybernetics that keep us on course, whether we like it or not, are governed by the innermost thoughts buried deep in our subconscious mind, programming our every move and propelling us forward.

Dr Maltz's book is a fascinating read. Learning about cybernetics has been invaluable for me so, if you can, I urge you to read the book.

Chapter Two
The Crisis

When one's partner in life betrays us, our reactions and emotions are universally catalogued in the following way, paths through grief and heartache:

- Shock, denial
- Pain, guilt
- Anger, bargaining
- Depression, reflection, loneliness
- The upward turn
- Reconstruction
- Acceptance, hope

Perhaps I suffered in silence but I did suffer. My heart did struggle under duress, it just wasn't the first thing on my list.

I listened. I wanted to resolve this and get through it. I wanted to survive with sanity.

I know that my sons said that if I had been weeping into a bucket, weighted down with the burdens of my dismayed and arrhythmic heart, buried in my diminished downtrodden self-image, they simply would not have been strong enough to deal with their own heartache.

I am deeply grateful for a relationship with them that has also taught them and permits them to be open and deliver what's on their mind honestly, kindly and with respect, however uncomfortable they may find themselves in their own relationships.

Witnessing the consequences of avoiding the truth, and the long-lasting effects on another, must be enough to dig out some courage and empathy and to speak one's mind clearly, with as much compassion as possible.

They are now twenty-nine-year-old men: does that make them old enough to withstand a crisis without expression? Of course not! Pain is pain.

What planet does that unevolved and cruel thinking sit on? People criticize and judge. It unsettles me. Age has nothing to do with the heart! To those whom I have heard saying "grow up!" I respond as a parent and as a mere mortal, but with compassion: "guard your words."

Other people's problems are private and so it is important to keep your own counsel. Friends should never be made to take sides or feel the need to pass judgement or make a decision that would disparage the other. They would be more loving if they stayed neutral and loved both – that's my feeling anyway.

I have learned a lot about my friends in crisis and that's good. It's not their reaction to my life that matters. What is needed is a compassionate presence nearby, a distraction from the uninvited, twisted onset of extreme and unexpected loneliness.

If we feel vulnerable and broken hearted, mistakes can happen because we can all too easily avoid our inner voice by listening to others.

Our closest friends are mostly motivated by some other experience – their own. Their opinion may be fair; it may placate; it may instil hope where hope may not have been anywhere in sight; sometimes, it may invite clarity. Sometimes though, none of those things are in sight. I remember one friend saying "well, you both looked so perfect together, lovely home, lovely children – just goes to show, too perfect!"

That felt like a hollow delivery of a beast of a comment, a worthless and cruel point to make, as though those things had not been genuine! An unnecessary measure of comparison and transference of their thinking and nothing to do with mine.

In crisis we are often at our best raw. With sharp thinking we patrol through each minute, let alone the hour.

I therefore rarely confide in these moments. I stay away from anything other than my own guidance or intuition because I'm humbled by a fear of the possible dissipation of my feeble strength and its extreme need to survive intact.

I must just say, I don't relish telling people they haven't got a grip of it or to kindly stop, when I know they are motivated from a place of support. It's just not always a welcome contribution.

The frameset that has served me well is to think how we can only ever travel on a single ticket in any event. This is a journey we take alone, in this sometimes-messy mêlée. It is tidy and much easier for the head. It is what I think of as avoiding war and protecting my sanity and mental health.

I did gratefully lean on the unfailing kindness and support of my closest friends who didn't overpower me with questions. I just needed to be left alone with my thoughts and they allowed me that. I am forever grateful to those friends and they know who they are. I love them – we are a tribe.

I also had two mini men to embrace, who woke every morning with their irrepressible joy and love of life.

There are those who did not help, some of whom I had felt were close friends, but it doesn't matter anymore. It is, however, a gloomy day when you find a friend was really a foe all along, with quite a different agenda.

Chapter Three
A State of Collapse

The first time I found myself crying silently, as I opened my eyes from sleep, was the morning after my husband's revelation. I was in a stupor. I was in a silent state of collapse, of shock.

This state is an imposition and it never leaves of its own volition.

To move forward, one must submit to the truth and then begin the upward climb back into a level of normality, of sorts. Warning: this may take some time!

In deceit, the veneer dissolves and the person witnessing this trembles, observing the stranger opposite them. I do remember noticing changes. I had put it down to other stuff, but I knew in that moment that he was not a man I recognised.

The second time I cried, I recall I was listening to music. I wiped my tears away quickly. The third was on a plane with my husband. I woke in tears and, if I'm honest, I felt rather stupid and rather pathetic. I didn't cry anymore after that.

I had no idea what I felt. I still hadn't moved on from the 'what do I do now?' moment.

I honestly hold to the premise that you simply cannot only like the good bits in your spouse or partner. The not-so-good bits need tolerance too. We are all flawed.

On some level, the mind of course shuts down when there is shock.

I was gathering a semblance of hope, to regain my full and comprehensive cognitive ability and composure. Honestly, I'm not sure I ever did that completely, but I promise I gave it my best try. It must have worked somewhat, because very dear friends of ours were stunned when I alluded to what was happening as a 'wobble'. They hadn't detected anything untoward at all and that was a top result!

The last thing one needs to do is destroy an atmosphere with one's own egocentricity and the then inevitable meeting of a zillion opinions, even if those are well-meaning ones.

To draw attention to such an important matter needs care – maintaining peace as its anchor.

I noticed his face break into a smile every time he saw me. I think that kept me going. It reminded me of someone who had once really loved me and would never have considered exchanging me for anyone in the whole wide world.

During what feels like the rage of disbelief, we all know that in such turmoil there can be a strange willingness to find a mitigating circumstance for the perpetrator. It may be the hope of quelling that pulsating longing, a craving to wake up from what might just possibly be a nightmare – just imagination.

I must be honest, no one wants to hear expletives about their friend's badly behaved spouse. That remains the privilege of the injured parties. I say 'parties' because no one swims free from the trauma and the grim and turbulent waters of a relationship careering into a gulley, whosoever's side they are on.

What becomes apparent is that one's own paradigms, one's own judgements are most naturally based upon personal and ingrained family doctrine and experience.

This is all fair enough, but there comes a time to defend one's right to decide and take responsibility for one's own decisions.

Here I will add I am at my most vulnerable when I'm aware of having to address the potentially successful, or disastrous, impact of my next step. Conversely, I am also at my most steadfast because that's when we need to abide by that old idiom and 'step up to the plate'. Raw self-protection kicks in and then so can courage.

I believe that when there is space to breathe, the next step has room to emerge and shed a little light on what feels like a dimly lit path.

Like the Pacific and the Atlantic Creeks, those parted

waters in the wilderness, we were on different plateaus. We were still engaging but swimming apart, treading water if you like, in more ways than one.

We had booked honeymoon suites for our trip around Africa: a bit sad, a little silly, rather ironic. I could still see the funny side of waking up together in these rooms, under mosquito nets with the sunshine heating us up. No telephone conversations were had with 'the creature'. I was told this was as a mark of kindness and out of respect for me – a generous offering. Looking back, I recall the many faces, the myriad dancing expressions on his face; I'm sure I felt at odds with myself too.

I also recall the sadness, punctuated with laughter and the fun we had, in the discovery of the places visited, in sharing the time together. We were charged by two hippo bucks on the Zambezi and fled in the canoe with an experienced captain, truly lucky to still be here to tell the tale!

Knowing one another so very well, the bottom line was and remains that we are friends without exception, supportive of one another when necessary and there have been times. We also feel gratitude for our spectacular sons, miraculously delivered via a first attempt of IVF.

One evening we were in Safari Lodge, having walked the whole way around the Falls. It was absolutely easy between us. To my utter awe, I recall spotting buffalo and, with an over excited and raised voice, I said:

"Golly! Buffalo at the watering hole!"

All the guests in the bar laughed! The bar was the 'Buffalo Watering Hole'. I kept my binoculars fixed when I saw a pride of lions. God had sent a white lioness, with her pride – a privileged and spectacular sight and my ridicule swiftly was forgotten. My key point here is do not blacken every memory.

Some years later, we agreed to leave the last twenty-four years intact. I did ask him to kindly admit any misdemeanours. We were brave, and in understanding the reasons for my divorcing him we respected our need to let go. He had almost been lost to a heart attack and I had a hand in his survival. It was life or death in more than one way. He had survived; now I needed to.

'After all, how often do we get a second chance?' – Jay Asher, *Thirteen Reasons Why*

I'm not sure we ever thought I would actually divorce him but, in the light of new clarity, one should never live without boundaries. I had no choice but to be responsible for myself, our sons and for the balance in maintaining the status quo because he was more 'at sea' than me… with greater burdens, admissions and upset. Disbelief was drowning almost everything around us. Neither of us thought divorce possible after many years of rubbing along so nicely together.

Chapter Four
The Truth Will Out & The Veneer Falls

Truth is important for respect, as a contracted life partner and as a parent. My words, verbatim, were "Level with me please; I deserve honesty." I felt dignified, justified and calm. He just stared, a foot from me. We were standing in the kitchen.

I remember our dog Willa was watching. Intuitive as they are, I remember thinking: she knows something's wrong.

He said, "You're right, let's talk… a glass of red by the fire?"

We were both becalmed (me and the dog, that is) for what felt like a stay of execution.

When we are teetering on the precipice of life as we know it, feeling cursed in whatever action we strive to take, we fear the impending carousel of reconstruction of our lives. In this case, it wasn't just my life, it was four people's lives.

I recall our drawing room at the time. The room was pretty, the candles were lit, the fire was laid and flourishing and the wine was a perfect temperature. We were prepped for 'The Talk'.

In that moment, I recall looking to my right towards the fireplace and its roaring logs; to our wedding photograph – so pretty in the loveliest, hand-engraved silver frame. I'm not sure where that frame is now. He was talking. I was out of kilter.

Strangely, in looking at that photo I sensed relief. Perhaps I was comforted by the false sensation of denial that the person opposite me was a stranger.

I would normally have left the room if I'd felt that uncomfortable or I would have addressed it head on, but the photo stabilised me. I was able fleetingly to recall all the good bits of this man I had been married to for eight years.

He was a man truly steeped in kindness and empathy. He always treated me with concern, kindness and respect in his touch and still does. Actually, he treats everyone like that, as his father did, as my father did. Opposite me in that moment, however, he was someone I didn't know. He looked unusual, neither smiling nor grim. He seemed sedated and off balance. His posture appeared lopsided – I felt awkward for him. He was exposed. His eyes darted left and right, from me his prey and back again; he embodied a snake. Whenever he spoke of someone he didn't trust, he would always say,

"He is a good man or he is a snake." Of course, this is but a light-hearted metaphor, but certainly I didn't know him at all then.

I kept focusing on our wedding picture, reassured that the man opposite me was just a visitor. I observed him out of his skin, staying silent. There was no hiding place.

I felt sadness and shame equally. I didn't need to speak. He was experiencing a level of torment. It was stunning to observe it as an existential crisis. I was hypnotised.

Intermittently, I averted my gaze between the photo and the fire and sipped from my glass. I recall I struggled to swallow – I suppose it was anxiety beginning to rise within me.

He obviously felt it important since he said this new relationship offered him a chance at "something unique." The awareness that I could see him in all this mendacity may have felt like a dramatic fall from grace, but I'm not sure if narcissism took him that night, because while something certainly held him in firm grip, he probably felt nothing at all, save the simple justification in serving his own needs.

Incredulously his talk began with, "This talk… is not about you. We, that is, not you and me, but us."

Them!

I steadied myself. I recall the ambience of the roaring fire. He added the incredulous, "We are moral people." And then, shortly after, the stranger left.

Chapter Five
A Deathly Stupor

Recently, I felt the same stupor draw me in when my mother died in my arms, and again at her funeral. It was a floating in and out of body experience; I imagine death must feel the same. I am sure the body protects itself by shifting into what feels like another dimension entirely, to avoid harsh and burgeoning pain.

Two spears to the heart. I felt equally extinguished by them both.

> *'The spear in the other's Heart*
> *Is the spear in your own*
> *You are he*
> *There is no other wisdom*
> *And no other hope for us*
> *But that we grow wise.'*
> – Surak, *Star Trek*

I can say that was stunning. One word, like an arrow, a spear at a target, shattered all my resistance. It felt like a crystal goblet, smashed to smithereens, broken into a zillion shards of fragmentary pieces.

With a smile, he said, "We have talked about marriage… but I haven't promised anything." That's all it took to strike my heart dead, fell it like an ancient oak tree, once magnificent in its stronghold, I was done and dusted.

As he left, he turned on the doorstep and said, "What a tragedy it is that this has happened, it is too sad."

I said, "If so, then why go?"

"I'm packed. I need to know what this is. I need to know if this is meant to be," was his reply.

Et voilà ! I sank into a heap.

I would obviously still be there if he changed his mind. I had no other choice but to hold the fort with two babies. I had to carry on. He, on the other hand, was having a crisis and asked me to understand. Not to put too fine a point on it: he said he felt a disgrace, and I felt disgraced.

People chastise the stance of the victim. I understand there is always responsibility wherever we may find ourselves but *sometimes* there are factors greater than ourselves to consider.

One such factor was the driver for me to write this book. We were (and I include this, as it was part of our wedding vows) to 'bear one another's burdens'.

Love, of course, changes and goes through stages. It mellows, shifts, sometimes it can disappear entirely, or at least be elusive. Until there is management of the relationship with the other, whose own needs may perhaps not have been fully met, it can often, no, almost always, dissipate.

Finding happiness and peace in life post-divorce signals a healing from what is often called a 'living bereavement'. When you finally begin to embrace that happening, you are slowly but surely setting yourself free.

Revering and caring for the memories is the key to not destroying your life by living in the past. It can be excruciating to begin to accept the challenge of a new life, but that is the work and what it amounts to.

It can take time to see how gracious life is – even when we feel we are in disarray. We feel upset, unjustified, troubled, maybe burdened and not wanting to put one foot before the other, forever remaining glued and martyred to the cause.

A life can seem as though it's simply been cast away. This is not about blame; this is just about owning up to the feelings.

We must handle ourselves with kid gloves, accept we are fragile but still valuable, and look at the goodness and at how far we have come, even in small steps.

We will find a new path.

Having forgiven ourselves for not living up to a

dream we once had, or given everything we had for it, we can wake up with hope in this new adventure.

We are responsible for how we teach others to treat us, tough as it sounds.

Others may choose a different route and it is paramount never to stand in the way. Our response and self-respect determine our next step, into a life easily as fulfilling.

When we understand that we need to tweak our self-worth and recognise our value and decide to start again, then we have built our boundaries; then life can begin again.

Chapter Six
Halfway There

When you apply for a decree nisi, where the court does not see any reason why you cannot divorce, there are one of two decisions to make.

Write off a marriage in ten steps, providing ten reasons for your wish to leave the marriage, or write out the premise, the story of the marriage.

I chose the latter.

The first option demanded I disparage the man with whom I had chosen to spend my life, the father of my children, in a sweep of ten paragraphs. Suffice it to say, I refused.

To dishonour every memory of twenty-five years with someone I still choose to speak to, who remains a trusted friend, who makes me laugh, who cheers me on and protects his family and lives for his children would be unthinkable. It would be an ignorant and inconceivable way to behave.

Some people didn't understand and saw this as weakness. I disagree. On love, I understand the love of the ecstasy, of the intimacy like nothing else that has gone before – the words, the softness, the freedom to express, the tenderness and rapture. "Boom!" There is a part of your heart that is given away and I believe, after this opening of your heart, it no longer belongs to you.

You gave it and it's gone. Someone once said to me, "Please don't waste a minute looking for it." I have never forgotten that. Sometimes, it gave us such beautiful things that we can never forget. If there were children, even pets, a love for the external family that we felt were ours for a while, then we know the value that was borne of that love – we are lucky. I also understand the way sickness may seep in and bloom into a 'Sissinghurst Garden' – full of energy, heavenly scents, rapture, the earth imbued with moisture and every nutrient needed for growth and strength and for life-force that somehow can turn dramatically inwards, into life threatening disease.

It is not possible to be full of this focus, of self-destruction with intensified and amplified depths of darkness looking only backwards, reliving the past and expecting that to fulfil the present with a life force.

There are two ways of seeing it:

The first is forcing darkness to obliterate the light…

'The soul in the darkness sins, but the real sinner is he who caused the darkness.' – Victor Hugo, *Les Misérables*

The other is forcing light into darkness…

'Darkness cannot drive out darkness; only light can do that. Hate cannot drive out hate, only love can do that.' – Martin Luther King Jnr., *A Testament of Hope*

I'm not sure you want to be alone – sure, you like to 'be' alone and often we are content in solitude, but to not share dreams and touch? That cannot be a way for anyone to live out their life. One could commit to the Lord, but to be locked away from human touch – one would still crave another's arms, another beating heart as recognition of existence. When you need to reach out to comfort or seek comfort, it is for warmth, not for the answer, not just an illusionary sum of the total. In that, and in every moment, we alter, and in a flourish change colour, and so the moments move. After all, an open window can throw a random rainbow of light, and in that instant reverberation one's lover's arms can be thrown into a dance of expression and pure momentary wonder just at the day out there – just at that! That is what it is – it is just that. A momentary stilling of the journey and so, yes, our feelings in that moment are real, but what of that? They are transitory.

No moment, no thought remains the same – verily, we find that old adage is true. So in their purpose, these thoughts stir us into the next thought and so on. The pleasuring of the mind, body and soul is infinite in two and feelings of the heart pulse may never dissipate – there is utter wonder in that. Our love is present still, where we left it once, in men or women loved, in the hearts of strangers and friends and family, those long before us and then after; those far beyond; those in spirit who continue to shape and turn our heads, who attempt to guide us by waking us up to the moment. This never changes.

One feels wonder that the caverns of the heart can be filled to the brim and yet it is infinite; in 'The Room' for ever more. One cannot fathom pain when the memory is numbed, immersed in forgiveness, and that is a key to love's omnipresence. A world inside us that pulsates and expands for all new things – so that our living is endless – must be the sensation we feel as happiness; the discovery of the new, where we fill our place and become even more. Surely it cannot be satisfying looking backwards and only defining ourselves by our past and our heritage? Emerging once more as new, with better things to learn and share, must be the definition of taking part and living and loving – so it is to redefine and refine ones heart, by finding and sharing love.

Don't stand still. No, don't be alone.

Chapter Seven
The Domino Effect

Divorce can feel like a game of dominos… one trip-up leads to the collapse of every domino, of all that we hold important. It is a collapse of the value of the energy, the commitment, the heart and sinew; all we gave to our marriage and to our family.

We had always been an incredible team. I am not a dependant or motivated by attachment per se. I took my vows with trembling heart standing at the altar. I recall the enormity, the dignity of the promises we gave. Importantly I should add that I relinquished so much in leaving that marriage that day and that I mourned in solitary confinement that day too, a long, long way from another soul, in private.

'Smile and the world smiles with you. Cry and you cry alone.' – Stanley Gordon West, *Growing an Inch*

I have always been told that I can cope and halt the panic. Perhaps, this is an abuttal from me, a definitive stubbornness. If I'm honest, I don't want to be run roughshod over in anyone's crisis so if you're like me, climb aboard your steely raft.

However, here I was in the crisis of my life and on my knees – a natural response to a dramatic revelation. I wept, but somehow, I understood it wasn't me crying at all, I felt like an onlooker. Any weeping was happening on its own. I would sleep and wake to a damp pillow. There was no movement, no gulping, no shudder. There was no even breathing or disturbance, just tears. Perhaps my soul felt suddenly awash with it all. Tears felt as though they came from the entrails of my being, somewhere deep, deep down.

It was as though I was sitting in my theatre seat, in the stalls, concealed in the darkness. The spotlights burning on the stage lighting up this person. I was there, I had a ticket. I can't feel my heart, my mind, I thought; only my tears run. I can't feel anger, can't assert the blame even. I can't feel anything.

There was an awareness that I was the voyeur. I assumed (if I assumed anything at all and, if I did, it was much later) that the pressure built up to the brim, burst like a dam and flooded over. Songs are sung of this. Songs I listened to then and still absentmindedly now, their words still pierce me. Shock causes all manner of muddled thinking.

I do have another admission.

I think I wailed (quietly) and hyperventilated in turn, a few hours after the 'revelation' (in solitude of course). I can say that I believe it is the soul that weeps and have thought about this a lot. I am sure the soul needs to ebb and flow, during a moment of twilight or, as it is often called, 'the dark night of the soul', when things ping randomly to the surface, like disturbed shadows dancing.

Chapter Eight
Why the Soul Must Weep

In all my years of friendship and the sharing of challenges with trusted warriors, I have come to realise that the shedding of tears is a fruitful and necessary journey, as is the discipline to stop and acknowledge that the release has been fulfilled. Waterfalls must be given time to ebb and flow. I know now, and I'm sure it isn't a revelation to anyone, that when one gives one's heart away, it is irretrievable. Love is, we know, an immense gift.

There is a compelling need to speak the words out loud. To express that magical feeling that can come over you suddenly. It's a treasure – a gesture as valuable, maybe more valuable, than anything, even more magnificent than the wonders of the world, the creatures in it and it is given by the force that created it, that created us all.

It chimes from a place that we had no idea was

teetering on empty. A place that may as easily be filled to bursting in an instant with a pure energy that is divine. It is an intangible gust of joy, propelled towards and through us, against which we have no power,

The greatest hardship must be then to let that person, that love, go.

No harsh feelings, just because they love differently to us. Just because they express love in another way, it doesn't mean it's of less value.

There are those with a checklist for their ideal companion. I had a friend who listed their partner's foibles and then boldly sat them down to address and demand change of those things if they wanted to stay; unsurprisingly, they fled!

What makes us who we are is imprinted in us long before the stabilisers come off the bike.

We can function, assuming we are always right, repeating the same challenges, even arguing the same points as our parents, driven by their own disciplines or, as the case may be, the lack of discipline implemented in their own lives. Perceptions on money, parenting, treats, diet, sickness, humour, success and attitude, along with a myriad of subjects including race, creed, education and all manner of tribal ritual, can all be inherited and thrown into the mix.

So how do we wake up and challenge ourselves to shed those indifferent paradigms, which include the hurt and the heartache? The loss and true lack of support can feel stuck there, built steadfast into our basal and cellular character.

We can choose the company we keep. We can choose the books we read. We can choose to believe we can re-emerge as ourselves, lighter and less weighted down by the opinions of others. This is a process, often lengthy and often a lonely one, so programmed are we to follow the crowd.

People facing life threatening disease often say at recovery, what a blessing the onslaught was! Surely, if we are listening keenly as we go about our lives, heeding the writing on the wall, observing the words we use and send out, aware perhaps of what gives and subtracts from the feeling of happiness inside, we might feel more at ease, putting deposits into an escrow account entitled: health is wealth, health is happiness.

If we work towards the understanding that, despite others not belonging to our tribe, they do hurt the way we hurt, laugh the way we laugh and mostly adore their children, striving to be the best they can be, getting just as lonely and afraid, feeling the same pain in separation from those they have given their heart to and received love from; if this is so then would our judgement not benefit from a tweak or two?

Most of us never fail to recall a kindness and, just as keenly, never forget a wound – when emotions are stirred, we never forget. Talking of wounds, everyone talks a big game on forgiveness.

It's a torrid path, when we are the walking wounded expected to survive against all odds, when we are feeling feeble.

It is the only route. The heavens open and the waters part when we navigate through what amounts to the well-documented shimmy through the eye of the needle, but we are assured how wonderful the gifts are on the other side.

Something happens when we forgive. Many (including me) have experienced this. I am sure of it. Something in the heavens releases everyone in the mêlée. When it is done, we hurtle downstream set free, accepting our loss and relinquishing the false 'survivor' status. Only then are we free to begin once more.

Getting there can seem like trudging against a sandstorm in a desert. The deafening yet silent noise with sand in one's eyes, sans sustenance, sans water.

Everyone experiences this at some time – everyone. Forgiveness, mostly of our own mistakes, makes it easier.

The hardship of letting go and redirecting ourselves to live within our best nature, that's the work, the pain.

We tend so easily to assert the blame outside ourselves, as though nothing can ever really be our fault.

We only carry these burdens because someone else slotted them into our psyche at some point, when we weren't old enough to discern or say no. That is true, but how damaging all that blaming must be to our mindset and to our bodies, notwithstanding our relationships. Falling in love, and moreover being in love, is the finest balm. It heals as it gives and cuts as it flees.

When we give our hearts there's no changing the mind. It's done. It was a gift we recall giving unconditionally. If we left it back there, accepting it may now feel jumbled, might we deter the dis-ease that is borne of bitterness?

The understanding that this love should surely encompass the flaws of the other, as much as the cherished bits, is something important to consider.

The understanding that we do not always get our own way or should ever reasonably so demand is another. The understanding that we are out of control, and that the only control we may monitor is our own behaviour, is fundamental. Failing this essential piece of wisdom, taught to me by my late father, risks solitude of our own making.

The dignity with which we live is rewarded, in like sum.

When we shed our tears, they must be shed in our private and personal truth, with abandonment, thus protecting our emotional and physical health.

The concept of caring first for oneself can feel so alien. Women building boundaries against the world can feel odd. After all, woman was created as the mother, the empath, with innate and authentic concern for others whomsoever they may be.

Woman is all things to man and child. How unusual, then, to have to build boundaries around her, when she was created to encompass life and not to reject any part of it.

Evidence abounds everywhere now, with profiles for each disease. Creating our boundaries out of respect for our fragile heart and soul must then surely be a priority.

There is a respected belief that wounds are the roots of mental and physical discord. So, perhaps we need to care a little better for our spirit since we alone are responsible for how we react and respond to our sorrow and our joy.

Chapter Nine
Victory or Defeat, Your Choice

When I was younger, my mother told me to be careful in choosing whom I might marry.

"You may marry someone for things other than love. If you do this, you must pray very hard that true love never beats its way to your door, ringing a bell in your heart. If this happens, you must pray for strength to ignore it! Know that you can talk yourself into and out of love and, if it's not pursued, you can pray that the love chiming stops, that it is extinguished. The consequences of your decisions are yours alone and will determine your life."

That meant that my life amounted to the thoughts I was amassing and that they were unstoppable and transmuting into my future. She also told me never to blame a man for curtailing my freedom, to do everything I aspired to, before settling down. She felt that marriage and motherhood were a sacrificial existence (however delightful), meaning I'd subordinate my life, putting myself last.

She told me to travel, to do everything I wished, forsaking nothing before I settled down to a life where my role would blend into Managing Director and there is quite a lot an MD does to be honest.

I married at thirty-one years of age, I felt twenty-one. I loved my work and my life.

I didn't take for granted I would marry – it was the farthest from my mind. What I didn't ever contemplate was that conceiving children would be an obstacle. I had been the chief babysitter growing up. I loved children, and still do.

In her wisdom, to recap, these were my mother's directives:

- Never blame a man for curtailing your freedom.
- Do everything you aspire to before you settle down.
- Marriage is a sacrificial existence, however delightful and means you subordinate your life, putting yourself last.
- Marriage creates a vastly different life and it is a privileged union.

I'd say that's pretty near the mark.

The miracles of our children, despite years with our vision blurred by exhaustion, are the most exacting yet glorious years. Our children were the ultimate privilege and had been tricky to come by. Our twin sons were miraculously conceived on our first attempt at IVF. I was a walking textbook, according to the brilliant Egyptian microsurgeon Hossam (Sam) Abdalla, at The Lister Hospital, Chelsea.

Sam Abdalla is a man so deftly able to read a couple and the possible pressure brought to bear on their longing for a family.

Some found they simply had to address they didn't have sex, an obvious obstacle. There were those couples that didn't want children but felt familial pressure to prove their infertility, which feels like self-punishment at its worst.

After delivering two boys, I was asked to counsel those looking at IVF. I sent countless women to Dr Sam, who said I had an inordinate amount of faith in him – I did. I had faith, full of respect for the heartfelt brilliance he communicated so sensitively to every woman and couple longing for a child.

I knew my thoughts and had the discipline to understand that the success of bearing children was also down to me listening acutely to this superb microsurgeon: so advanced, a leader in the method at that time. I recall the national outcome in 1992 for IVF was around 7%, Mr Sam Abdalla's success was 17%.

Sam demanded my understanding and told me that my mindset was important, allowing him to take guard over this process. The 'gift of life', as he framed it, needed my trust in him and the preparation to relinquish and hand over full control. Looking at his research of me, Sam told us we would have a child. We could succeed, but only as a team. I was to put my concerns, my fear of not having a child, for my partner, for me, of not giving my parents, parents-in-law, a grandchild, of feeling unfulfilled as a woman... Sam said, "These worries should be put in a box with a beautiful ribbon tied around it, on a shelf but out of sight." If we were to conceive, he needed me, us both, to be calm, rested, and to hand over the baton.

Once again, I understood the responsibilities my mother spoke of. The ultimate gift of a child would be a glorious and blessed space, where I would reside happily, far, far down the list for evermore, sleeping unreasonably lightly, ready for anything from a baby's nightmare to a midnight call and adolescent crisis, to my child's heartache and its limitless power. So, my mother was right. Find and pursue your freedom first, establish who you wish to become, where your life will lead you, be courageous, be brave. Nothing meant for you will ever miss you, and everything not meant will evaporate and eventually disappear. It was sound instruction, from someone married and a mother at twenty-four, who did not have the freedom women have today, who excelled and loved her career as a Coloratura; she remained forever flamboyant and forever an inspiration.

Chapter Ten
Retain, Never Detain a Soul

The mother of one of my oldest and dearest friends, Maggy, a worldly and glamourous, beautiful woman with four daughters and a son, whom I have always loved and admired, taught me, with mischievous smile to, "retain a man, never detain a man." So, I never have. I hate to be detained beyond my will and suffer suffocation easily; I give my word and that's it. When I'm committed, I don't need egging on and putting in a corner, it feels like sabotage and mistrust. I respect this saying wholeheartedly. To chase anyone will always have a negative effect. What a pearl of wisdom Maggy gave me! Allowing the other person, particularly in conflict, the space to reflect and be is a mark of respect.

Speaking of conflict, if one is in the midst of it, to wait for one's cognitive reasoning to emerge is prudent and an extremely good idea.

Stay calm and, if possible, always turn your back on

harsh judgement, however justified you may feel in that moment. Until you have gathered your thoughts and given them time to emerge into a coherent message, make no stand.

Goodwill is important, for the sake of your health, family and future – so is compassion. In any battle, strategy is key. Paused communication may calm a torrid sniping and a tormented opponent sitting opposite.

The message is to hold on to your self-respect, be less ego-centric, have dignity – then, despite your position, you will have a voice. The broken-hearted do mend.

We all have a responsibility to preserve ourselves through our actions, without filling every minute fit to bursting with retorts, served carelessly and without the consideration of impact.

There is always impact and a reaction, a beginning and an end. Know with certainty that you receive in turn what you put out because there is no hiding place. Every book, every personal development directive, stems from the 'manuals'. For Christians, this is the Bible, but each religion in every corner of the world acknowledges the directive to think before you speak.

On reflection, like most, I treasure the nurture of peace and silence. I'm a bit of a party lover and yes, I can talk! Sometimes the space I'm in is filled with music, sometimes I talk things through with a trusted person, who accepts my flaws – a true friend.

To occasionally luxuriate in solitude; to reflect and restore without an inner voice champing at the bit; to just exist, that is everyone's given right and it's heaven!

My father would tell me to ease back from striving saying it was fruitless without relaxation and rest. The employment of a little humour, particularly during times of tribulation and woe, was key for me.

With that understanding comes the justification of the explanation I gave when asked where my husband was. I deflected and delivered a cheeky, irreverent retort.

Quipping, with furrowed brow, I made light: "I fired him."

I was not disparaging anyone and, more importantly, I was retaining some humour. I felt I was proving that my head was not in that bucket. Further comment was unnecessary, everyone laughed and that was that. It wasn't impolite or a nasty lemon-lipped remark.

In laughing, I stifled any need to speak further about it. It was effective. I felt it deflected from my pain and killed gossip. I didn't express anger, was not turning into a bitter, whining, chubby old bat, toothless from eating too much chocolate.

Transferring the blame outside myself would also quash my confidence to ever sink into a strong man's arms again. Anyway, the instant laughter deflected an awkward moment and maintained my dignity by way of an inoffensive remark that people still find amusing.

Heartache is all too frequent a malaise amongst those who love deeply.

I have always cautioned myself to never misplace blame. My feeling, on some level, was that there was responsibility from me too for the outcome of my marriage that I needed to atone for. On a more important level, this crisis was not just mine; it also belonged to our children. I had an epiphany. I decided I would break the spell, the wretchedness of the paradigm that I had played along with unknowingly, the one that grew me into a person who expected that men could not be faithful, even the most loving and kind men.

My father, father-in-law and husband were all fine men, great fathers, but they were unfaithful, so were not all men the same? This muddle seeped into my subconscious scripting – I finally woke up to that.

I could blame my mother's incessant wrangling and punishment of my father, but I shall not, even though I watched how every jibe eroded his happiness.

I witnessed an encompassing erosion of joy when he read or sat cross-legged like a young boy, watching the flames striking the logs in the fireplace. It was so terribly sad to see, a sort of palpable hopelessness. He said he understood the longing to relinquish responsibility and just wander through life alone.

It would seem it had begun to erode any innate contentment in his life.

My mother had made the decision to move on, after

discovering his dalliances, but she never let it slide and just couldn't bite her tongue. It was a vain attempt to preserve her so-called stance of forgiveness. It was over-bearing and ugly, as any argument becomes over time; one without respite.

It would seem that despite changing his life, remarrying his PA (sorry, but "yawn…") then later seeking solace in our home, since they were disparate, he still had no hope of recovery from a seeping sadness. He was a sentient human being, loved by all his family and siblings and me; for us he was a dear heart with little blemish, much less flawed than those who chastised him. He was never afforded the room to begin again with her trust in tatters, but that was because her hurt encompassed her, had broken her already fragile confidence and courage, as it sometimes can. There really was no let-up. She didn't want to forgive him, my feeling was she knew not how – she topped herself up with bitterness like petrol in a car, filling up readily, fuelled up for the next rush of her disappointment.

For the next thirty years she carried a heart that bled unforgiveness; despite a warm and fun-loving veneer, those that knew her well sensed she was inconsolable – she had only ever loved one man.

It could be ugly when it surfaced, like a tumultuous wave that from nowhere at all rises so high as to terrify and move and rock the very foundations of the oceans, before crashing to the shore, finally petering out into calm, dissipated wrath, dwindled to nothing but quiet, lapping waters once more.

My mother simply took no responsibility for her emotional life, her world; she gave to others without a care but starved herself.

I know that her unforgiveness kept her 'his'. I remember she would ask me, "What will become of me? Where shall I be laid to rest? Will I be with strangers in the large Swedish graveyard, will there be a friend there? Perhaps I may be with your father, at least we know the best and worst of one another then, I would not be afraid or alone anymore."

She is with him. They are together and there are no more memories of heartache; I feel sure they are friends once more.

My siblings disagreed, even though I said I would acquiesce to any decision they may have made if they wished her to be laid to rest elsewhere and pay for the process. I wanted to know there would be a formal burial and where that would be. For over three years, they remained unresponsive and there was no progress. In the end, it took four years and church intervention for the vicar to finally call me and say I could come and take her home from their vaults; she had rested on the same shelf as Ingrid Bergman had once waited until the papers were in place for her to return her beloved Fjällbacka in Sweden.

Apparently, I was the only signatory on any

certificate, her only carer and next of kin. My mother's dearest friend, Pia, accompanied me – I broke down on every visit to the church, for four years. I was inconsolable; distraught that I could not lay her to rest respectfully as we entered the fourth year since her death.

I had promised I would pay to inter her and pay the costs. The church also offered to contribute; it was a desperately sad and frustrating situation. I had done everything I could to peacefully settle the muddle.

The Swedish vicar had laughed and said, "You are the middle child and so am I. You became a mediator and I became a priest."

He was gentle, a natural empath, and despite his kind tolerance I am sure he was tired of it all. It should never have been the job of the church to police my sibling's behaviours. I was upset for the church, who are quite busy enough without such wrangles.

I had considered taking her to Sweden, to her parents' grave. It would have been complicated but doable. But when I asked her closest friends their view for counsel on this possibility, they disagreed quite passionately. "England was your mother's home for fifty-six years; she'd want to be here. How would you visit her grave if she were in Sweden? She must be with your father."

So… there we are!

The church approved, her cousins approved, her best

friends approved and so, she is with her first and her only love. I feel, quite truly, that she is content and at ease now.

The Swedish Church approved the division of her ashes, which is forbidden by law in Sweden. Because my parents had lived here in England for such a long time, I asked them to consider this so that my siblings could also have a grave to visit. I asked the Swedish vicar who conducted the ceremony of interring her ashes in December 2020 to kindly send a packet of ashes, church to church, to my sister's local vicar. He respectfully did this for us and her ashes were officially and correctly laid to rest. Goodness only knows so many urns sit in garages and cupboards forgotten and I did not want this to be the outcome; people get busy and forget.

Chapter Eleven
Two Masterful Attributes

I have learned of two important attributes of human nature. The first is that we are all called to be sacrificial at some time. The second is we are called to compassion – neither of these qualities may render a jot in return. Compassion sits just beneath the surface in all of us, so nothing unusual there. As I see it, it's an unrequited act of empathy, as the native American proverb reads:

'Before you judge another, walk a mile in his moccasins.'

Those that serve as a way of life do so because they are gifted in these attributes and not necessarily because they are martyrs, or 'do-gooders', or even selfless. They choose their profession because they are drawn to it and feel compelled and happiest within it; it is not a hardship. It is a natural calling and they naturally excel at the task. These people are made in a way that expresses their pleasure to serve with naturally patient love and humour. Of course, if one sits them down and asks, "why this profession?" there is usually a good and clear reply – they all have good reason.

These humans are rare. I have come to stand in awe of the way they manage the once independent, now totally dependent, patients that to varying degrees need constant reassurance. All too often, the residents are emotionally impoverished and abandoned by their families. It is shocking to discover the evidence of how rarely members of the family visit care homes.

Chapter Twelve
Forgiveness is the Force Behind Survival

The strain of infidelity can impress upon a life, but so can surviving torture, being shot at in war, losing a child, living with violent inhumanity and much more. There is no need to extrapolate. The aftermath may leave us hollow and struggling for survival, afraid and justified in needing comfort from those unique individuals I have mentioned, with the compassion and education to care.

Then… there is forgiveness and what it could mean.

'The weak can never forgive. Forgiveness is the attribute of the strong.' – Mahatma Gandhi

'Forgiveness is not an occasional act – it is a constant attitude.' – Martin Luther King

'Resentment, it is like drinking poison and then hoping it will kill your enemies.' – Nelson Mandela

'I wondered if that was how forgiveness budded, not with the fanfare of epiphany but with pain gathering its things, packing up and slipping away unannounced in the middle of the night.' – Khaled Hosseini, *The Kite Runner*

'Forgiveness is not about forgetting. It is about letting go of another person's throat. Forgiveness does not create a relationship. Unless people speak the truth about what they have done and change their mind and behaviour, a relationship of trust is not possible.' – William P Young, *The Shack*

My father had an affair and I recall my mother convincing herself that she had no part to play in that tangled web. I don't doubt the reasoning. His irresistible need to respond to a beautiful woman in his midst was what she called 'his condition'. Outwardly at least, that helped her never to blame herself.

Forgiveness means letting go and starting again. I'm not sure my mother ever really felt brave enough until just before she died, when we went through her 'terror barrier' together. She said she felt forgiving would leave her just as she was, "standing like a child alone in her socks" ('strumpläster' in Swedish). She would be at her most vulnerable. She felt that any definition of her would flee, without her 'tag' as a 'wronged wife', forced into difficulty by her husband, with her identity stripped.

I felt a sort of hopeless compassion – there was room for gentle hugs; I held her hand, I held her a lot. In the last days of her life, I climbed into bed with her and held her like I once held my babies.

No one ever needs to be told what to do. Help can simply mean being there silently in the background and not in the way – just within whistling or whispering distance, staying in the sweet spot of temperance. I could empathise with her fragile stance, but I argued that it was not to hold her prisoner. If I may be honest, to give up on re-establishing her life by staying so sad was heart-breaking to witness but also wholly unacceptable for her wider health and the reason for its dwindling existence.

Ma lived with me for the last five years of her life – I began to know her once again.

It was my privilege.

I had left home at seventeen as soon as I could. I loved the freedom. Thirty-eight years later, she was living alongside me in the little wing of our home. We had the chance to meet again, this time as two women, not just mother and daughter; it was also fun.

I had been a very independent child. My mother said after the age of three I no longer demanded anything from her; I think I didn't crowd her. My brother was three years younger and my sister was full of beans and latterly announced she had ADHD. In my late teens, my father would beckon me home each weekend and if I didn't come, he would get agitated. I told him they had created a daughter strong enough to stand on her own two feet and shouldn't they be happy that I felt secure enough to leave, knowing they were both my stronghold and my rock?

Chapter Thirteen
Hidden Signals of Deceit

My father, as eldest son, was called back to Sweden to manage the enormity of the machinations of the sale of the family's international subsidiary back to the American HQ. It didn't help his case that he agreed to the task before consulting his wife, but such were the duties to his father and the greater family's interests.

We three children were in the British schooling system, which operates quite differently to the Swedish one. My parents couldn't find a co-ed boarding school and although both had boarded, due to distance-driven needs (Sweden is so big a country that travel to the desired schools can be an obstacle), they had never envisioned their own children living away from home during their formative years.

Without question, my father took on the task as his father bade him and, understandably, my mother was upset. He had agreed to oversee the sale of the family's organisational part of NCR to the original partners of my great grandfather in Dayton, Ohio, USA.

Pa proceeded to commute to and from England for two years. In that time, he also found alluring company that he should not have yielded to. His lover was known to the family, a former girlfriend of his brother's, and that went down very badly indeed.

Interestingly, my father was chastised for choosing the position which placed the greater family's need over his wife and three children – so he seemed damned if he did and damned if he didn't. Ideally, he should have spoken with his wife and discussed the decision. Things may then have been easier. But he didn't, and breaking this to my mother implicated her self-worth, obliterating it with the ease of a guillotine.

So, my father was chastised for agreeing to the position before consideration of his wife and children's needs and my mother was similarly scolded for neglect of her husband and putting her children before her husband. Lose, lose and no win! Of course, what happened to my mother was that, in my humble opinion, she began to propagate a magnificent disease inside, fed by her bitterness – I feel sure Parkinson's began early and burnished into her eighties. The sourness settled within her, like the juice of a lemon hydrating her body, it could be biting. Still, she appeared to cope.

My father was reminded of its sour presence often and so, like sand through his fingers, his love ran away.

Those two misdemeanours, her best friend's flirtation and the Swedish companion, left his wife broken.

Chapter Fourteen
FEAR: False Evidence Appearing Real

My mother defined herself by her experience. She didn't want to let my father off the hook, even after his death, even after more than a decade. When she died sixteen years later, she had found it in herself to forgive him a smidgeon enough to have visited his grave – she exclaimed at how beautiful the private gardens were. He rests there beneath a Dalecarlian birch.

My mother would ask me often, "Christel, what will become of me?" I would simply try to reassure her and say, "All will be well in the end, you have my promise."

Her unknowing made her afraid. Her disjointed belonging made her sad and insecure and I was sad with her, as children often are – mirroring their parents' emotions – an expression of their compassion, which is an expression of love.

My parents had been lifelong sweethearts. He never stopped loving her, he said so. In loving him, she never let go of her anger, that chord never failed to strike in her. I feel I understand now that she feels safe and content alongside him.

It is reverent to look after the deepest wishes of those we love with all our heart, even those hidden wishes, as my mother thought hers were. Even though she is not *in* her blessed ashes – her soul is in heaven – the ashes are a symbol and a requiem of her life. I often visit my father's tree; now I go often and am with them both there, under the Dalecarlian birch.

Chapter Fifteen
The Allure of My Father

Since it was I who disclosed his flirtation with my mother's best friend when I was ten, that paradigm may have set itself firmly in my psyche (albeit shoved down as far as it could go). Most men are flirtatious around women, does playfulness always have to mean infidelity?

Her friend would turn up when my mother was absent and go straight to my parents' bedroom, and it truly bothered me even when I was only ten years old. I wanted to scream at her: "You want to be with my father and dare to come to our home when my mother is absent? You are disgrace!" But I was never brave enough to say that. No matter how hard I tried to quell the anger and indignation, it stayed with me.

In my naïveté I felt compelled to talk to my mother, and at no point did I consider that I would be responsible for breaking her heart. I had never witnessed such an unfolding and instant collapsing of a heart – a torturous expression of pain, an alarming combustion of sorrow. I was so sorry.

Many of us have experienced such shock alone, without any clear way forward.

My mother and I never spoke of it again, but if we had, I think I would have held to the premise that the truth is everything and I would choose to reiterate that again and again, feeling that ultimately it had been the most respectful gesture toward her.

'Anything is better than lies and deceit.' – Leo Tolstoy

And talking of truth, when it happened to me in my marriage, I was felled like an oak. I learned pretty sharpish that I was sitting opposite a stranger and plunged into an abyss. Avoiding my gaze, the impending admission was palpable. I knew what was coming. I expected him to ease me somehow, definitively, into absolving the blame. I didn't say anything at all, I couldn't. I was silent, becalmed, stranded like a boat without wind. He seemed to be in freefall, incapable of gauging a reaction; perhaps it was my frozen, emotionless mask of a face.

Inwardly, I was paralysed with the fear of an imminent delivery of a Bouncer, the most aggressive and threatening ball in cricket, targeted at the throat.

Could an onslaught of feedback from me even have

been possible? Could I ever muster to emit an explosive reaction? I didn't, I couldn't – I was just holding on. It would have been a first to have been punchy; puerile from me, even. It felt more seasoned of me to listen and remain attentive. Anyway, who knew what to do? Not me.

We each react individually, plus I'm Nordic and, generally, the Scandinavians do not come unstrung in dispute. I felt poleaxed, like that oak tree, in one fell swoop. Everything in my mechanics was called to a halt. No sudden rush to attack came.

Like a glacial Swede from the wastelands of the frozen north, I didn't come unstrung.

We are very direct. We don't scream and threaten death; this calm reaction is not contrived and must be somewhat of a relief to those within earshot. It may be culturally learned behaviour, perhaps a bit of that and a bit of God's grace that I pray for daily to please rest about my shoulders.

One might consider the history of the beating into submission in 878 when Kind Alfred, after famously burning the cakes, defeated the Vikings at the Battle of Edington. The Viking Age was considered vanquished in 1066, when King Harald messed up at the Battle of Stanford Bridge.

The Scandinavians blended thereafter into the peaceable and solution focused peoples we know them to be today.

Chapter Sixteen
The Glorious Subterfuge That Is Motherhood

Here we were in our precious home. The delicious aroma of comforting peace hanging suspended in the air. The balance of that safe place where no judgement presides. The support of those there, who give and receive a simple and assured love. The sigh that comes with a closing of a door against the forays of a frantic world supported each one of us, and we lay outstretched in endless and fathomless support of one another. But that was then and now was now. Welcome solitude.

I can recall it instantly, since feeling is the single attributable factor to any lasting memory, and as I write, I should not be surprised that it re-emerges here. The sudden worry that I was not quite able to fully fulfil that precious balance left me destabilised, undermined and weakened. Knowing the partner of the household was now going to be detained elsewhere was impossible to rationalise.

Martyrdom here is not intended, please do not misconstrue. I am just stating the fact that I didn't lay myself down as a doormat but found myself as the singular 'head of house' and this is an overriding, haunting memory of that time and it lived on and can reoccur still.

This is also for every mother who is married to a devoted but nevertheless 'busy' father. Mostly, we put our own needs last; truly we barely remember what our needs once were.

P.S. Obviously, and to the men I have loved and who have loved me back, who have been faithful to me, I do know that not every man out there is unfaithful.

I include my precious friends here too, those whose trust is built as the foundation of our relationship, because…

'To be trusted is a greater compliment than being loved.' – George MacDonald

I spoke of it recently when a man asked me what I wanted from a love in my life. I said, "Someone to meet me on the bridge, who shares his burdens, where I feel at ease to share mine. I think I am a little tired of being the only responsible one and I do have a longing to sink into a strong man's arms, it feels lovely."

He said, "You need to be looked after now?"

"No, he doesn't have to be my saviour, or have every

answer, but he needs to be able to say – I'm here, I'm with you and you know I'm listening and, God knows, I do love you too".

Chapter Seventeen
The Interloper

Honestly, to receive emotionally abusive calls (from whom I now call 'the creature') from midnight until four a.m. – twenty-three calls in one night, was brutal. Only an insane woman deliberately unsettles another woman. Silence and heavy breathing; it obviously gave her some kind of thrill and was predictably received as a threat. The police were reassuring and kind when I called them.

They had been keeping a record of her number dialling ours. I reminded myself of that. They said, "Christel that's why we are here, at the end of the phone, please try to sleep." They were empathetic, strong and kind.

Those perpetual nuisance calls were astonishingly brazen. Wilfully stepping into rivalrous combat with someone else's wife and the mother of two small children, to win her husband and justify her ghastly behaviour, displays narcissism.

The interloper worked in the same industry as my husband and his diary was visible to her. The thrill was to intimidate and unsettle me. I'd had a call from the radio station co-producer saying I was not the first but rather the seventh woman whose marriage she had attempted to infiltrate. I admit, I was thrown out of kilter, which was of course the aim. I had two small children. I would have gone through hellfire for them. I wasn't afraid but definitely, deliberately destabilised; I kept my head. I also became fully aware of the muddle the creature was in.

My youngest brother-in-law urged me, in no uncertain terms, to speak her language, "Tell her where to go, she won't respond to anything less!" I waited, not wanting her behaviour to influence mine, but did as he suggested in the end. I demanded her number and called her. She said, "I'm not going to have an argument with you or debate, so don't even bother!"

I said, "I do not need, nor do I value your view. I don't care about you, the air you breathe or the ground you stand on!" These words were how I felt, they were also the cruellest words I have ever delivered, but I needed to disarm the person on the phone, the enemy.

This served to silence her. I added that it was never too late to look in the mirror, knowing she was certainly capable and indeed worthy of finding a man of her own.

"The police have recorded all your calls to this number for the last six months. Stop now or suffer a criminal record and add an already pending harassment order."

I asked her to express some grace, to wait until the marriage was resolved and added that if she were the one, he would find her. What can be worse than the endless ramifications involved in meddling in someone else's marriage? Before I put the phone down, she thanked me for talking with her.

It took three years to get her to yield, to finally cease her bullying. Listening to her abusive voicemail messages frightened me.

The police forbade any contact with her from either one of us. In those days, we had no internet, call holding had only just been developed.

In fact, the creature was known then as 'call-holding' by her colleagues. She apparently had no qualms about telling the team whom she had set her sights upon. There was an obsession with my husband. I think the abuse on the answer machine and the unpredictable behaviour helped in a way; the truth and unconsidered behaviour from her began to sink in. I had no anger, I wrangled through it with God. I hope I didn't bore friends with it – I don't know the answer to that.

It was that I was responding as calmly as I could with only immediate responses. I didn't know what was coming next.

I'm inclined to call this experience a spiritual attack. When we are feeling broken, there can be a chink in our armour that unwittingly may allow an inroad for attack. When we are so bludgeoned into a drama, sometimes we get stuck and see nothing else. Indulging in this pain can so easily become an addiction, fortified by the justification we feel for our wounds.

Eckhart Tolle in *The Power of Now* writes:

'The past has no power over the present moment.'

Well, try telling that to someone trudging through the flames, wondering whether the next step will lead them to collapse or embolden them – when you are there, you don't know the outcome, you can be surrounded but still you feel alienated with fear.

It is tricky not to embrace the past, having no power over the present, during the devastation of heartache. Tolle also writes:

'Some changes look negative on the surface but you will soon realise that space is being created in your life for something new to emerge.'

Well, that space can take a hell of a lot of time to emerge when you're feeling stuck! Tolle adds:

'Sometimes letting go is an act of far greater power that defending or hanging on.'

Whatever you fight, you strengthen, and what you resist, persists. The ego says, I shouldn't have to suffer, and that thought makes you suffer so much more. It is a distortion of the truth. The truth is you need to say yes to suffering before you can transcend it.

We may easily begin to identify ourselves as a victim of circumstance, and what is worse, others may begin to believe that we have been pushed into this and identify us as helpless and worn, which of course, we never are.

Chapter Eighteen
Gratitude Magic

Mostly, we can and do recover. Once we have dusted ourselves down and reconvened with living, which in my experience happens when we are reminded that the world (remarkably) kept on turning, then we are through the worst. We are blessed when we realise one day that we have survived.

One of the best suggestions ever shared with me, in my attempt to let go of the debilitating diminishing of my self-esteem, was to try to practise gratitude. It sounds a bit silly, but I can assure you a ten-point gratitude list is life changing.

The first time you begin, it looks a little like this: I'm so happy and grateful for…

1. My health.
2. My family's health.
3. My safety.

4. My family's safety.
5. The roof over my head.
6. The people who care about me.
7. That I am beginning to find the strength to move forward.
8. That I am beginning to allow myself to step away from my unhappiness and address that this is my responsibility.
9. That I am learning and enjoying a new chapter in my life.
10. That my sleep and health align with these wishes.
11. & One for luck, that I remember always: the only obstacle between success and failure is persistence.

Once you begin to create this new habit, it has an undeniable impact. Somehow with gratitude, I felt a restoring of my personal power and my confidence. The truth is, unless we are woken from the stupor of feeling shot down to a small remnant of our former self, we continue to sink deeper into resentment. A small change of behaviour by way of writing a daily gratitude list can dissipate the risk of one's whole existence stuck forever, down there, in full bloodied resentment. Having bitterness as a new and vibrant life partner may in the end amount to living half a life, one that unwittingly beckons in disease. These days we are more enlightened than ever on the impact of stress and inflammation, of how the body absorbs what lies in our subconscious mind. How cortisol, the hormone that triggers the fight or flight response, is managed, or rather unpacks and disconnects the body's support system, leading directly to a dumbed down wellness. Our body's reaction to cortisol is purely down to our lifestyle and our choices. It doesn't have to be this way – it is always worth looking at studies on this topic.

When we are at ease with temperance and grace whispering guidance in our ear, then we have found a new path. The opposite decision, to remain disengaged, can have us careering down an escalator to a dungeon from where the strength to set one foot before the other, let alone to clamber up a ladder and start living again, can appear out of reach.

Looking only backwards, reliving only the past and expecting that to fulfil the present with a life force that supports us is, I can confidently say, impossible.

After the event, it leaves trauma that allows inflammation and discord to spread through every cell of our body, submitting us to a life that not only destroys joy, but forces those once supportive friends and family to abandon us to the frozen chamber we have chosen to live in. That is why people do not heal, the depleting of our goodness this way is the fastest route home: ashes to ashes, dust to dust.

Chapter Nineteen
Peace Vanquishes All – One of the Universal Laws

God knows in that moment I learned that Peace is the Warrior – The Conqueror. These days I witness this as an accredited mediator in ADR, Civil & Workplace. Unsurprisingly, I have stayed away from family mediation for the time being, a period of respite is sensible.

We all wince at the thought of facing someone in dispute. The fear of rejection is recorded as every human being's greatest fear. We all want to preserve our better nature that puts ourselves in the best light. I do know it takes guts to choose peace. I also know release is quick to follow when we try and then we find we walk away with greater ease, starting a new chapter without shame, with the dispute settled.

I have learned that you don't need to punish anyone for anything in this life. I recall the principles of cause and effect as one of the seven Universal Laws.

A little about these seven laws 'at a glance' via The Proctor Gallagher Institute:

1.The Law of Attraction. In short, a connection between your feeling, what you attract to yourself and the results you get in your life.

2.The Law of Perpetual Transmutation refers to energy; thoughts are energy and so any idea or image that is held in the mind and nourished must move into physical form. This law explains the creative process and more.

3.The Law of Rhythm. Everything is in constant movement 'to and fro'. This law governs the movement of all seasons, the ebb and flow of the tides and the reaction to all action.

4.The Law of Relativity shows all things are connected to one another, high or low by comparison, with those above or beneath them; we make everything positive or negative, high or low, by comparing it to something else.

5.The Law of Polarity focuses on the opposite of all things, both sides of a person or circumstance. Every up has a down, hot-cold; good-bad; inside-outside, left & right.

6.The Law of Cause & Effect explains action and reaction, that they are equal and opposite. This impacts your relationships, the respect you earn, your income etc. Being aware of each action ensures you reap what you sow, your thoughts transmute into reality and every cause has an effect.

7.*The Law of Gender* is the Creative Law. This decrees that everything in nature is male and female, both required for life to exist. In the animal kingdom it manifests as sex. It also manifests in the mineral and plant kingdoms. All new things merely result from the changing of something that was into something else that now is, a caterpillar to a butterfly, a thought into physical reality.

Once there is understanding of these laws, they will impact your life and you can become a conscious creator of your own reality. There is focus of these laws in this book – the steps to finding peace after divorce. As I always say, keep an angel in your pocket.

Chapter Twenty
Cheated and the Cheater

I have just been reading up on the cheated and the cheater – it's awfully dull! So much is whisked up in 'blame culture'. It has little to do with listening to the precursor, or to what happened in the first place. So little advice or guidance is given on how to manage one's inner balance, of how to let go and how to move on. In my opinion, most jump onto blame.

Even if asserting the blame outside oneself is convenient, I still believe it is short lived and weak. And so, now I'm feeling all 'patched up' and almost beautifully whole again, I am enthusiastic that I can make some sense of my journey and share it with you.

When I fall in love again, I hope never to be cheated upon because my boundaries will be a sign of my self-respect. I have begun to choose my 'tribe' carefully, particularly through this Coronavirus period that has granted us all time to reflect upon what truly matters to us, who truly matters to us and why. Who cannot have addressed that when so much tragedy, heartache and fear abound? We need to care to unite with those who share the same moral compass, whose thoughts about life and its challenges dovetail with our own. I am of course, probably like everyone else, afraid to be hurt, but I always try to be brave.

I am sure we cannot dodge love and its richness or the deprivation that comes when we expect too much from it. Not so the narcissist, who only concerns him or herself with their own image and their own life.

So often there are signs or 'red flags' that we ignore in the hope that they will vanish into thin air, but they never do. We must choose wisely, listening and understanding who that person is, respecting our differences and meeting on that bridge, equal in our care and concern for one another. We are all of us vulnerable to heartbreak, but we can mend. Bitterness is something we must fight against and live without.

Divorce can be considered a living bereavement. It has the power, as in our case, to unfold and fracture the whole family. It is for each of us received quite differently and individually, but with as bold and as callous a strike. In a world where family can be so easily eroded, where parenting is paramount to the stability of our child or children, it is unacceptable to disappear into the dark waters and the billowing clouds of one's own trauma. We all need support and understanding to break the spell and live with one another with sane and sound mind, even if our partner chooses a new path. It's a choice within our clasp and one that can halt a living bereavement in its wake.

Me at age six and a half, engrossed in my painting

I was a child once!

My father, Carl-Johan Arne Holst-Sande

Me and my mother, Eva Margareta Lindahl Holst-Sande

The nest was sweet: me and my siblings

My grandmother, Friherrina, or Baroness Märta Af Verchou

My great grandfather, Johan-Emanuel Sande

My great grandmother, Wilhelmine

Contentment after collapse

Three loyal brothers in arms: Julius, Ben and Fabian

My mission to harmony accomplished: Fabian, Chris and Julius

Me and my boys, Julius (left) and Fabian (right)

The future is bright: Fabian and Julius

Remembering one's value – if I can do this, you can do this!

Chapter Twenty-One
Precious Friends

I feel strongly that friends should never feel they have to take sides. They should never be asked to make a decision that would disparage the 'other', or feel the need to pass judgement, or indeed serve a view at all – just staying neutral and loving both shows compassion. I know from experience how valuable this is; it is kind and comforting.

Asking what one might need, how one might help, feels so much better. Never to be forgotten is so kind. A negative and downward spiral, without the presence of empathy, can lead to depression. A good and solid first step in support would be to ask a few questions.

I needed privacy, but felt consoled by the presence of others, in another room. It wasn't because I was balking at sharing my innermost thoughts. I just needed peace and to hang on to my dignity and a semblance of sanity; to immerse myself in being awake and feeling alive, despite the death of my marriage. I escaped the opinions of everyone learning of my demise by calling dear friends living in Sarasota. I explained I was struggling with a situation and needed space.

They simply said: "Just come."

It was also respite from my adored mother-in-law, who was already arranging 'visitation dates' for her grandchildren at her home!

I recall when I took our little boys to friends in Sarasota we were welcomed with open arms, which was so generous. They didn't enquire very much and were so gentle and careful with my feelings. I couldn't find the energy to coherently share how I felt; it worried them a little that I was bottling up my thoughts, not wishing to be a burden, but strangely, I wasn't bottling anything up at all. I was simply stunned – that state of mind held onto me for seven weeks! I was treading water. I relinquished control and tried not to analyse.

On leaving for Sarasota, I asked if he wanted to drop us at the airport. I added that if he hadn't worked it out by the time I returned, I would leave the marriage. I wasn't intending to make him 'walk the plank', it just jumped out of my mouth all on its own. My former love was then at home with all the rope in the world. Coincidentally, we were selling our house, so all doors were ajar. There was time to reflect, change a path; there were no roadblocks at all for him and no excuses for indecision and, with that open door, sun blazing in, freedom was an open invitation

The boys went into a morning nursery; I got a gym membership and hired a car. There was sunshine, ocean, sand beaches and calm. My friend's youngest daughter celebrated her birthday with the sweetest party and so the boys had new little people to play with. I am forever grateful for that precious friendship – it was comforting and extremely generous of them to have us there.

I watched the boys playing in the sand, running into the sea, giggling and free. I felt profound relief. It had been a good move to get them away from the 'wobble'.

Children are extraordinary energy receptors and so there is no hiding place. Daddy rang his boys each day to say hello, so their lives were harmonious. I recall thinking that in leaving home I had let go; given up on the increasing and inevitable tension, on having to plan the visiting dates my mother-in-law wanted and generally having to jostle with everyone's concern and opinions. I was suffocating. The infiltration of everyone was backing me into a corner. I am a free spirit. I have great respect for boundaries. Going away helped me through this, the greatest crisis of my life.

I recall my sister rang me in Sarasota, to impose her views…

"You must ask yourself *why* he sleeps with another woman when clearly you're available to him?"

It was a typically worthless comment; it deigned to undermine me and felt heartless. The intimacy between us in our marriage had always been healthy and unrelated to this, that is what made it all so difficult to grasp. I had learnt that my father's love wasn't diminished for my mother, not that I could get my head around that immediately; he told me his infidelity wasn't a reflection of her, but of himself. I still wasn't sure I could believe him, even though I looked deep into his eyes. I've learned so much since being left with my own reflections and meditations and the memory of his exact words.

My sister's opinion lacked compassion. Often people have a compulsion to meddle, or to be part of the drama, rather than to listen and support. To offer a useless and frankly cruel jab, wholly lacking in concern, when someone is at their most sensitive is crass.

Choose your tribe carefully. At all costs I would say keep your own counsel; useless comments can often lead to a sharp detour headlong into a muddle, caused by a wagging tongue.

Chapter Twenty-Two
Revisiting the Manual

Someone said sweetly that if I had trouble sleeping, or any worry at all, I should look at the Concordance at the back of the Bible and that I would be led to a line that would stretch out its hand in comfort. I found this Psalm when I looked up 'Fear of the Unknown'.

How I leaned on the words. Here they are…

'If you say, 'The Lord is my Shepherd'
You will not fear the terror of night, nor the arrow that flies by day…
For He will command His Angels concerning you to guard you in all your ways.
They will lift you up in their hands so that you will not strike your foot against a stone.
You will tread the Lion and the Cobra.
You will trample the great Lion and the Serpent.'
Psalm 91

I whispered those words in my head a lot; they were a great source of comfort; they rocked me in their arms. I told no one at all, in case they thought me heading into madness with the Lion and the Serpent.

Likewise, Psalm 23 felt so powerful for me:

'The Lord is my Shepherd, I shall not want, He restores my Soul.
He guides me in paths of righteousness for His name's sake.
Even though I walk through the valley of death, I fear no evil for you are with me, your rod and your staff, they comfort me.
You prepare a table before me in the presence of my foes.
You anoint my head with oil, my cup overflows.
Surely goodness and mercy shall follow me all the days of my life and I shall dwell in the House of The Lord.'

I would sleep leaving the Bible open at that page. Someone told me it would protect me, that if the devil was in flight, looking for vulnerable people to bring into his domain, he would sigh, sending his eyes to heaven and say, "Well done, God, you got there before me!"

'Satan trembles when he sees the weakest saint on his knees.' – William Cowper, 1731-1800

It felt comforting that these words of the most powerful psalm wafted over me as I slept – it alleviated my stress and my grief. Any doubt entering in would scurry out unwelcome… like the devil might scurry, tail between his legs, with no air to breathe in the sanctuary of the Church's promise, even if he attempted to enter through the so-called 'Devil's door'.

When you are alone in a house, with two little people and a dog, with such a big empty space around you, there is comfort in daring to reach out. I have learned that prayer has increasingly supported me and helped me to determine healing. I would say this works for those with a wavering faith too.

Religion per se is less important than the private and personal conversations we may have with God, or our inner, finer self, whomsoever and howsoever we perceive that to be. It is private.

I reached out in my aloneness and felt rewarded in that sense. I could keep it to myself.

Most of us are aware of something greater than ourselves, maybe we simply don't consider it. We may find ourselves in nature on a mountain top, on a moor, gazing up at the Milky Way or awestruck by the Northern Lights, or the birth of our child, when we are suddenly brought to our knees by the magnificence of our existence and the feeling of our own insignificance, quite simply as tiny atoms, and finally the realisation hits us that we are merely mortal.

'The total number of galaxies in the universe seems to be in the region of ten billion and each of them has about a hundred billion stars, the size of the sun. These numbers are so absurd that I find myself in a good mood, there is so little I can do to make a difference, it feels liberating.' – Erlend Loe, Norwegian novelist, screenwriter, film critic

Who knows, we could gain so much more by not...

'Leaning on our own understanding – are we really so smart, or so wise?' – Proverbs 3, 5-6

At the time I couldn't think clearly about where to go now or the best way to pursue the solution with any semblance of sanity. I didn't dare contemplate the collateral damage; I didn't know who to listen to... It felt as though I was in a pulsating stream of opinions; a continuous, relentless echo. I stopped talking about it and this gave me peace and space to be calm.

This is just a recollection of a journey; it is not my intention to evangelise at all. I believe we all have our beliefs and no one may interfere without invitation.

I am reminded of William Holman Hunt's allegorical painting (1853-54), *I stand at the door and knock*. In it, the artist deliberately painted the door as ancient and overgrown, with no external handle, to represent the problems of a closed mind – the handle of the heart is on the inside.

I do know that if we need to call out it is okay and we are heard. I do find the humility of the painting powerful and believe there is more than a little hope within it.

My father prayed. I knew more of that towards the end of his life. I have his daily prayer; it is simple and I share it here. He was often troubled and fearful:

"Dear God, help me to restore my life into balance, so that I can be happy without worry, to keep going. Thank you. Amen."

After my father died, whilst sorting through his things, I found a letter he'd written to the Archbishop of Canterbury. He respectfully asked him to groom himself and remove his beard. There was a stamp on the letter, but it was not my letter, so I did not post it.

My father found it offensive, the beard bothered him so – golly it made me laugh! He obviously felt there was a subliminal message the archbishop was conveying. My father found that quite unnecessarily ego-centric and felt that in such an elevated position the archbishop should be respectfully presented and groomed correctly, after all, plenty have beards and they already know they are welcome in church.

I asked my mother if she ever prayed and she said, "Yes always, in thanks for the roof over our heads, but no more. I am far too far down God's line with my list. I'm sure he's grateful I don't disturb him when others need him more."

That reminds me of Jim Carey in *Bruce Almighty* – a favourite film of mine. As God, he was deafened by requests. Apparently, that is most people's belief – that we mustn't 'bother' God or the Holy Spirit. My understanding is that's not how it works.

The truth is my mother didn't ever want to understand the mirroring of the Old and New Testament. She couldn't grasp Revelations and definitely would never have been interested in textual science or theological theories, or any such academic matters. My mother still took the sacraments as a matter of course, with respect for the Swedish Church in London, who were her extended family, and I know she did call out in solitude.

Erik Lindahl, my mother's father, Judge and Sweden's Chief of Police, professed to being an atheist and yet he read the Bible every day. He was a friend of Edvard Munch and Harald Klinkoström, highly acclaimed artists. He was an intellectual gentleman, a scholar who played the violin and viola, piano and smoked a rather elegant pipe, which I recall smelled delicious! Morfar (Grandpa) wore a beret on the top of his six-foot-six slim frame, which was faintly embarrassing for me (I found it feminine however flamboyant). On Good Friday, 'Long Friday' as it's known in Sweden, he fasted – the whole family fasted. Black was worn and the home and family were quiet.

On the following day, 'Black Saturday', or as some know it 'The Harrowing Hell', the family were in a respectful state of mourning. My mother said she and her sister Helen read or drew until Monday.

My grandfather bore out quite some actions for an atheist. I don't know for sure, but I do understand that as a man of law, impelled by justice, he found the Via Dolorosa and the crucifixion the most extreme, contemptuous dishonour and illegal trial in history. To slaughter a young man of thirty-two years old so brutally, a man inclusive and conveying only peace who had committed no crime, was unacceptable in my grandfather's eyes, and the reason I believe he bowed his head and prayed on his knees, in sorrow and respect.

His legacy is the reason I find myself in church just before Easter each year, for the 'Stations of the Cross' service, feeling incandescent and saddened for the hideous horror bestowed upon this young man called Jesus.

I'm sad that I never had an in-depth conversation as an adult with my grandfather; I never heard his inner beliefs or understood why he argued so much with God. I believe that he was probably much nearer to God when enveloped in debate than he ever realised. Is it not an affirmation of the existence of God to protest so vehemently as an atheist? Why not just sit on the fence questioning, or simply stay agnostic, open to learning, staying teachable?

He was my 'Morfar' ('mother's father' in Swedish), had a twinkle in his eye, a strong Skåne dialect from Southern Sweden and many talents, such as popping his violin under his chin whilst holding his knife and fork during dinner, ready to play as he devoured a mouthful.

This good man entertained us as children and we simply adored him – never too grand for a silly and a jolly; these remain precious moments.

Having retired to Palma, after many years widowed, he fell in love again and married in his dotage – at eighty-two, Erik was inspiring. Aunt Jean (Giguère), as we called his wife, had an American accent and an infectious humour. My grandfather bought her silk lingerie and she floated about in it I recall, looking so delicately feminine.

I also remember my mother smiling at my father, eyebrows raised (in pretend shock) at her father's gifts to his new wife, with a whispered "impressive at his age."

Aunt Jean told us gripping stories that were scary. Her English family had traversed 3000 miles of open North Atlantic Ocean in 'The Mayflower' voyage of 1620, spending two miserable months battling against strong westerly winds before finally arriving from England, by way of mis-navigation, into Cape Cod Harbour.

Mesmerising and full of hope at the same time, she was an accomplished artist as her deceased husband had also been an artist of note. They were two widowed and lonesome people, my grandfather and Mrs Giguère, now no longer alone. They had found one another – life was sweet.

My 'second father', my father-in-law, was a soul who raised himself. He was a diffident, cautious man who understood and breathed in the human spirit. He was also the only white man, or man at all, to whom, not so long ago when apartheid loomed heavily, other nations would speak. This was a man who united all those he came across. Simply, he loved everyone who loved his beloved sport: cricket.

He was sweet, a gentleman who on greeting a stranger would introduce himself quickly (in case they did not know him) as he took their outstretched hand. I found that gesture alone heart-warming and unforgettable.

His parents had 'done the right thing' in leaving him to be educated in England at a tender age. He was sent 'home to safety'. His parents returned to India, his birthplace, to their tea plantation in Bangalore. This was the norm for many children then.

He was a gentle and wise human being and his father-in-law adored him as his own. Such was the strength of his faith that he was drawn to the church and juggled the desire to be ordained, pitted against the demand and the gift and the fateful role he would hold within the world of sport. He possessed a compassion and an uncanny ability to read people. His respect for the power of cultural and, more importantly, cross-cultural appreciation supported and affirmed his communication with others and, may I add, they loved him for it.

The posts he held were dedicated to the wider, international family of unity that sport brings, cutting through cultural misunderstanding. He called sport 'the great leveller' and every one of the family has that ringing in their ears. His oft singular childhood built within him a tenacity to overcome differences, as he dedicated himself to the sporting talent bestowed upon him. He believed sport to be that incomparable leveller between all and a unique way to unite and find common ground.

The Spirit of Cricket, a directive written by him and edited by Ted Dexter, was a guide to the code of conduct within cricket that would further serve 'The Sport of Gentlemen'. These guidelines are upheld now and endorsed by every international cricketing nation. The invaluable contribution he made by almost singlehandedly bringing South Africa back onto the world stage of cricket not only knighted him, but honoured him as a Peer of the Realm, a Lord.

It was with tremendous pride that he took on the role of Whip in the House of Lords, to continue his passion for sport and its undeniable ability to build routes between nations. He had an impact when he spoke, always with measured and deliberate caution; he was brief and to the point, a great speaker.

The Spirit of Cricket continues, demonstrating goodwill and peace amongst men. The love he imbued along his path was evident at his memorial service in Westminster Abbey. Every cricket captain of each school he had attended as a boy and young man, with every captain of every test team he had ever played with, for or against, travelled from all corners of the Earth to stand, heads bowed in respect with love for this fine man, alongside the royal representatives of the British Monarchy.

On one occasion, he invited me to accompany and to assist him as Adjudicator at Lords, for the upcoming test match – such was my in-depth knowledge (his words, not mine) particularly as a Swede, that he felt I should contribute my view to the selection of the Man of the Match at the closure of the game – he could be extremely amusing.

'The Outsider sees most of the Game!' – Proverb

Both he and my mother-in-law loved this expression, feeling it on point and accurate. Both made everything fun and, of course, I had a little cricket education thrown in too. A great family friend observed that the truth was I had been thoroughly 'ear-bashed', and that was quite near the mark! Converted, I have loved cricket ever since. In the cab to Victoria station after that fine day's cricket, he said, "I am relatively young you know, but my body, strangely is not."

I said, "Is it your heart that is fragile?" He had undergone heart bypass surgery some years earlier.

He replied, "Yes, I have broken hearts, but you do believe me when I say I never meant to?"

"Of course!" I said, as I held his hand

He wasn't a huge hugger, but he did hug me and gently cupped my cheek. He said, "You are also loved."

He was a man of tender heart and tender expression.

I recall he once visited our boys' prep school, Papplewick. One of our sons was playing for the Under Nines (U9's) that day – a fledgling at seven years old. The Headmaster, Rhidian Llewellyn, put Fabian into bat last on purpose, hearing his 'Grandpa Cricket' was coming to watch.

Seated with him on a bench I asked, "How should one show appreciation of a four or a six, a wicket or a catch?"

He looked at me, in all seriousness but sporting a smile and said, "Decorum at all costs – perhaps a gentle clap."

I said, "Right, I shall follow your lead."

Fabian hit the last ten runs needed to win the game! The lack of decorum oozed from every pore as 'Grandpa Cricket' whooped and squealed, jumping out of his seat clapping and shouting "hurrah!" again and again – it was hilarious! I, on the other hand, was tempered and (as directed) suitably tethered, in full decorum. He was adorable! He said, "These are the true test matches!"

I recall this great man's empathy.

On one occasion, during the crisis, I was sitting and looking out at snow falling outside, a blizzard. It was a picturesque, frozen Kent countryside. During this unforgiving storm of freezing temperatures, my sweet father-in-law called.

Worried for me and the two babies, he asked how I would bring in the logs from the shed for the fire and other such things. The family had floundered a little, they were concerned and had met to discuss the flurry of our mess. He told me they were upset, that they asked, "Did you worry about the logs, when you left us?" Frankly, it brought back memories they could all have done without revisiting – a resurrection I'm sorry was brought about, of wounds that may never abate.

Of course, it can be covered over, like a thin coat of paint. It may cover a smudge, but it may still emerge from a broken heart after many years with the slightest trigger.

I have noticed since I was very young that I could, and still can, easily discern the word in a sentence that is the embellishment or the untruth. I am sure the awareness of the combination of body language, tone, darting of the eyes and haphazard breathing all helps in the world of the natural sleuth! On point, I can hear the question, loud and clear…"So, Christel, if you are such an intuit, what were you doing hanging around until that point?" Well, it's a blameless point you all made and one that was fathomless to my children and closest friends, who didn't get it at all. I shall hope to articulate this throughout, perhaps then absolving the attack against my behaviour shared in comments that inferred: "You were a doormat, were you not?!"

Chapter Twenty-Three
The Fear in a Child

It is complicated and muddling for children if they witness a shift in the status quo when they play no part in it. No parent wants their child to have a moment's sadness. Perhaps some parents are so wrapped up in their upset that they simply don't grasp the impact on their children's security and how frightening it can be around a raised voice and such unrest.

I recall one of my sisters in law, a mother before me, saying, "One minute of fear in the heart of my child is too long." No calm, balanced parent would ever allow their child to be afraid. Maybe, when our own status is challenged as adults, we are not so brave either; perhaps we are just as fearful as that young child, trying to grasp the situation.

The effect on family and the way we deal with crisis will always impact us. It is a fact that 'we reap (most definitely) what we sow'. We need to be strong enough to think, to listen.

'Conscious Parenting' is worth aspiring to. Essentially, it suggests that the child is not the problem, but rather it is us, the parent, who first needs to fix ourselves. I absolutely agree!

I have learned that study and action, even if its uncomfortable, is the only way to effect change in the family; to take responsibility in the management of our family. Talking and pontificating as we do may release tension but action is the surest way to reveal and uncover the solution. Its straightforward I guess and, yes, easy to say. It takes a bit of 'chutzpah', but it is worth the discomfort to fight for what you believe in and, in the end, it brings the dividend and hope of safety and sanity.

The fear in a child has been a bit of a calling for me. I was young once. I agree with my sister-in-law, fear in a child can feel like desolation for a child, even for a minute. Reassurance that the family is safe and able to continue seamlessly, even if the parents live apart, is vital in developing the inner security of the child.

It may be many moons later that we recognise the paradigms we have been indoctrinated with, that we realise we can find, amend and delete, determining our own. It has been a major factor in the disciplining of my own parenting. Any problem with my small child is foremostly mine; I hold myself absolutely accountable.

Parents must hide their vexation at their own incapacity to address their role as parent, as the adult in the room.

'Give me a child until he is seven and I will show you the man.' – Aristotle

There is a responsibility to educate our children with consistency. Of course, they can be tiring and exasperating – as we can all be at times.

Parenting is a lifetime of responsibility – once a parent, always a parent. A valuable parenting trait would be to readily serve those we defend, with far greater ease than we consider defending ourselves.

Chapter Twenty-Four
Scripting Our Children

We are blessed to have our sons, who were both born via IVF, miraculously 'whisked up in a saucer' by the great man Hassam Abdalla at The Lister Hospital in Chelsea, conceived on the first attempt. I cannot imagine a life without their colour, their gifts, their omnipotence and unconditional love. To be supportive and to alert them to the pre-eminent value they have to offer is one of the most commanding and loving tasks I can give. In short, as parents, we must become the frame around our children's picture.

It is an overriding factor that each action and reaction we display is scripted in our children when they are very young. We are meant to show them the way, then… get out of the way. The expression 'do as I say, not as I do' first appeared in John Selden's *Table Talk* circa 1654. Just in case you misheard, this doesn't work, because children invariably do as we do and not as we say. My own view is a strong one. I do believe children are not just a gift, but a privilege. Sadly, for many parents, children are burdens that they could often do without.

'There can be no keener revelation of a society's soul than the way in which it treats its children.' – Nelson Mandela

'Hugs can do great amounts of good, especially for children.' – Diana, former Princess of Wales

'The survival of humanity depends upon educating the hearts of children.' – The fourteenth Dalai Lama

'The best way to make children good is to make them happy.' – Oscar Wilde

'If you want your children to be intelligent, read them fairy tales. If you want them to be more intelligent, read them more fairy tales.' – Albert Einstein

'The Soul is healed by being with children.' – Fyodor Dostoevsky

'Children are the living messages we send to a time we will not see.' – John F Kennedy

'If we are to teach real peace in this world, and if we are to carry on a real war against war, we shall have to begin with the children.' – Mahatma Gandhi

'Children find everything in nothing; men find nothing in everything.' – Giacomo Leopar

'It is easier to build strong children than to repair broken men.' – Frederick Douglass

'Children are not a zoo of entertainingly exotic creatures but an array of mirrors, in which human predicament leaps out at us.' – John Updike

For the love of our child, our egocentric view ought to also focus on the impact and reaction of the family. We must be awake and cautious, considering the way in which we script our most impressionable young children.

A child grows up worshipping the essence of the parent, absorbing their unique qualities, be they kind, indifferent, spectacular, creative, musical, calm, feisty or criminal, to name a few. This leads me easily onto the reason for my love of men: it is simply down to the formulae I was exposed to around my father. He was, of course, the only constant male presented to me growing up. It stands to reason then that I would marry someone similar, since this is a well acknowledged and logical thread. My father-in-law was bestowed with the same traits, the same gifts and, in part, the same burdens – or we might call them blunders. I recognised my father in him as I recognised those traits in my former husband and there's the rub! Even today, I hold compassion for every step taken on their paths much travelled, though therein now lies my assignment to be self-aware and remain responsible for my choices.

My father-in-law was so like my father – they were born in the same year, three months apart to the day, altogether beautiful and exceptional people. They were humanitarian, wise, empathic and deeply kind. My former husband was the apple that fell close, no… right under the tree.

I suppose if I were analysed, the therapist may deduce that it was my paradigm and ultimately my acceptance or even expectance that I should simply wait for my husband to be unfaithful. I have taken on board that, on some level, deep in my psyche, I may possibly have been complicit.

I do understand the power of paradigms and have studied this extensively. This is one of the reasons and one of the drivers for writing this book. I am not here to absolve anyone of the mess that poor behaviour delivers, or the trauma felt in those who innocently suffer in its wake, nor am I shouldering all the blame in my own case. I have considered all these points, almost forensically, as one does when one is in the eye of the storm, waiting for the onslaught of any premature, thoughtless movement that may be met with even greater density and backlash. We are all responsible for our decisions. After all, we can never truly affect another person's actions, unless of course it's through tyranny or torture.

It came to light that my gentle father-in-law was concerned that I would not manage to stay calm amid this previously unencountered and cumbersome misery. He called me daily, he prayed with me – that I would sleep, telling me firmly that I should, "Not get down in the dust and the dirt and fight, simply focus on the children and be gentle on yourself."

He had a faith, he was devout. A believer, he understood the power of prayer. I did too. I was grateful for his balm. I shall never forget it, because that is what it was, balm. I believe he offered me what is referred to as Agape love.

Agape love is selfless, sacrificial, unconditional love. It is the highest of the four types of love in the Bible. The strength he gave me through that love he showed allowed me to believe that I could manage this crisis, however fragile I felt I was at that time.

In my case of course the babies came first. My father-in-law was direct… "then comes the mother." He was praying with me with all his heart, praying down the phone that I would have calm, that I would be able to rest while the children slept, protecting them with joy and buffeting everything else away with peace as my bow and arrow, with faith and not indulging fear for one second.

I was ten when I chose to reveal my father's flirtation with her best friend to my mother. Could that possibly have stayed in my psyche for so long, never dissipating fully? Could the reaction she displayed have impacted me?

Like any child, I loved my mother happy, rather than angry or sad, but still, I knew she deserved to know that my father was having an affair with one of her friends. I also understood that if she could not muster taking any action from that revelation, then that was her choice and none of my business. I empathise because choice is a weighty companion. Taking action and shifting the balance, by addressing change of this enormity, was for my mother as torturous as visiting Hades.

When you have three children and you feel undermined and utterly sabotaged by the possible onslaught of consequences, how do you find the strength to emulate and answer as Jackie O did, and turn the other cheek?

I agree with Stephen Covey (1932-2012), American educator, author and speaker, when he said we need to embrace and brave our choices:

'Until a person can deeply and honestly say, I am what I am, because of the choices I made yesterday, that person cannot say I choose otherwise.'

Chapter Twenty-Five
Truth: The Abundant Blitz of Consequence

'One voice speaking truth is a greater force than fleets and armies.' – Ursula K Le Guin, 1929-2018

Truth is how I am compelled to live; it has marked me. I have always been truthful. It's not always easy, it can be extremely uncomfortable and not running with the crowd has never been a popular path. It was never a conscious choice, but I have always been driven by it in my work and in my personal and business exchanges.

My mantra is: The Truth Always Catches the Lie.

My mother did say she thought about my father's allure, that she always felt threatened by the attentions of every woman they happened to cross paths with. They would go to a party and she could scan the room in under ten seconds and identify the woman who would most look to catch my father's eye. I must add, he did little to deserve the attention, but he was handsome with a warm and gentle energy and, of course, he enjoyed it all.

He was young when they got married, only twenty-one, so the rush and thrill of attention from strangers was perhaps understandable, even if he was too immature to fully grasp the consequences of the dynamics and how it affected his wife. My father certainly didn't beckon women in deliberately, but he married too young. I have two sons, I don't urge or dissuade them, but I offer then same advice my mother gave me: "Don't blame anyone for curtailing your freedom, fulfil your dreams, travel, explore... before you settle down in marriage."

Despite it all, as an adult, I found a mitigating circumstance for my father's behaviour, not difficult since his mantra was "Always find a mitigating circumstance for someone else's behaviour. We all have battles but know it may be the projection of their inner challenges and not always a reflection of you."

My father taught me well. I became a little too good at turning the other cheek. No one gets away with anything in this life, but we must apply our boundaries and that means simply remembering that one's self-respect is as important as the other person's need for understanding when they lash out or mismanage their treatment of you. There is no excuse for venting on another without consideration. It's most definitely a choice. Let us vanquish the fear that may be inside us and around us but never forget that we are responsible for our self-control.

I look to my grandfather and his sometimes severe discipline of my father; perhaps that's why my father's confidence and self-esteem soared around adoring women: they raised his self-esteem.

Vanquishing our childhood paradigms is a valuable challenge in life that requires persistence. The truth is that we are, as we know already, programmed long before the thrust into adulthood begins.

I took on board that my parents' marriage was no business of mine. I would not allow it to reflect in the commitment and the love he expressed to me as my father. I was of the marriage, but not in it. I did a Jackie O and turned the other cheek.

Occasionally, I harboured a smidgeon of sympathy for him since my mother had her foibles. He was calm, whilst she craved continual attention. She was a beautiful and vibrant woman but she was dramatic and controlling and would interrupt conversations with somewhere between a B and a top-F note pulsating through the conversation during a lunch, just because she felt like drawing attention. She was dramatic, no coincidence that she happened to be a 'Dramatic Coloratura'. She would also pop two fingers in her mouth and wolf whistle, hailing a taxi at 500 paces, which she did once at midnight in Knightsbridge years ago after leaving a restaurant!

One only had to scratch beneath the surface though to sense her battles with her self-esteem. This was inconceivable to most because she was socially skilled and at ease around strangers and always a super hostess.

I must add here that there was never a moment when I witnessed an unkindness or cruel exchange between my parents. I could not take sides, something I knew my mother would have preferred, but I have always sought balance. She had told me that if they had parted when we were small children, she would not have sanctioned any visits from my father – such a stance has never been permitted in my lifetime at least and would have broken any devoted father.

I still shudder inwardly when I recall her tone, her face, her thoughts to misuse her maternal power. The punishment she wished to administer was fruitless, but it was cruel.

It was the most savage attack she could have levied against my father, just because she knew his gentleness and how easily he made us love him back. When they were divorcing, she couldn't fathom my neutrality. I was supportive of both. I managed everything she asked of me. I loved her, I loved my father and I never spoke negatively of either, to either, to anyone.

I recall she demanded I never speak with my father again and tried to ban all communication. I laughed out of shock. I was incredulous. It is so easy to judge and lose respect in such circumstances but there was a mild hysteria in the moment, so I just changed the subject and let it go.

Quite soon after their divorce, my father was rushed

to hospital and I rang to ask his condition. His new wife was his next of kin, so I was not permitted access to detail. I said, "I'm his daughter, I'm worried for him – he is so troubled at the moment, is he going to die?"

The doctor simply said, "Your father will be fine. It is anxiety that driving his heart to dip; he is not dying. I will tell him you have called and that you love him."

I have never forgotten the sweetness in his voice, the kindness.

I immediately rang my lovely GP, Dr Robert Lefever, and asked how best I might help, as my father had been arriving at my flat, unannounced and obviously feeling alone. Robert said, "Invite him in, let him be there whenever he wishes. He is travelling from Oxford to London; just allow him to be there and you carry on with whatever it is you are doing. He can read the paper, rest, go for a walk with you, make coffee, just be in your presence, you need do no more than be there. It is lovely, it is enough."

Robert was a friend as well as my GP and is a friend still. Our friendship began when he asked me to translate some medical studies from Swedish to English for his practice. I had a translation business called Crystal Clear Translations for the Scandinavian languages. He offered to pay for my work, I declined.

He said, "Okay, my dear, perhaps one day I can help you. Please remember – just call if you need anything at all." I did much later, seventeen years to be exact, once more in relation to my father's wellbeing. He said, "My dear girl, how may I help you?"

There are people in my life who have reached out with kindness and to whom I am indebted; their kind understanding has supported me in the spartan moments of my life. Writing this book has alerted me again to recall their generosity.

It is difficult to be an island. I'm not even sure how one becomes an island, but I became one.

Chapter Twenty-Six
My Debut in Court

My movements as mediator began early in my life. By the time I assisted in the machinations of my parents' divorce at the Royal Courts of Justice, I was twenty-nine. Evidently, I was the first person to be given permission to mediate their parents' divorce; this is recorded in the annals at the Royal Courts of Justice.

Having dealt with the division of contents and both solicitors, I didn't find it tricky at all. My father asked me afterwards where I had been and why I didn't intervene earlier. I did take umbrage at that because it wasn't my call. I had stepped in as soon as I was told that it was costing them a small fortune to see the divorce through. There was also a lack of confidence in both my parents – attending the High Court felt most undignified and shameful for both. In 1988 the cost of them being there was astronomical and due punishment for his inability to settle an agreement. The case had come this far because my father had not adhered to the planning of a financial split. His head was in the sand. He was certainly regretful. He didn't wish for his marriage to have unravelled this publicly, and his procrastination had set in.

The very kind QC acting for my mother forbade me enter the courtroom for what he called his 'Purple Patch', or the cross examination of my father. I shall forever be grateful to him. He gave me a bear hug and said, "You may be twenty-nine, but you are still their child. I, as a parent, will not permit you to be present." He was wise and an empath and I have never forgotten his quick thinking in 'loco parentis'.

Mediation provides a way through what may be the mêlée of dispute and the permission to disagree. There are choices to make in seeking resolution. In a dispute, you will be asked if you are willing to listen to your disputant, but you are not called to agree or disagree. Remaining impartial and not entering in is the only way to find a way forward.

'For fools rush in where angels fear to tread.' –
Alexander Pope, *An Essay on Criticism*, c.1711

Mediation has allowed me access to an immense service; I feel it is a gift. Our relationships are a crucible for peace. This is another driver for this book.

So many of us, untrained as we are in such conflict resolution, ever consider that our delivery of advice or critique stems from the seeping transference of those values instilled (no doubt imbued with well-meaning) in childhood by those closest to us.

As a Swede, so deemed different, I developed a need to find understanding quickly and, to some extent, I would mould myself into the 'crowd' to survive the endless scrutiny and pressure of my classmates. I learned the nuances and took the banter; I was calm, refusing to take sides; managing debate was an area I developed and found relatively easy.

I began quickly to discern the strong from the vulnerable as I was definitely highly sensitive and quick to critique myself, so I was striving never to remain neutral, but rather to empathise in the midst of chaos. Unsure as to how to calm a situation, bullying being rife in an all schools, I discovered the power of a division of fairness in what can often feel as desolate as war. The permission to speak without judgement gives room for reason, little by little. It also gives time for thought, almost always attempting to circumvent the injury of pride. Fast forward to when I was permitted, as I mentioned, to step in during my parents' divorce to mediate – goodness knows I had no idea what the definition of that was then!

I loved them both, was a child of their marriage and had, in my mind, simply no right to comment, react, or to side with either; as they say, I was of it, but not in it. My siblings took on all manner of unentitled roles, which were not called for, merely adding to their heartache of the loss enveloping us all.

Mediating the sad end of my own marriage, I was so conducted to preserve and not damn and blacken wonderful years and precious memories. People around us laughed at such a possibility, but we were and still are loyal on the key levels and we didn't want to inflict what would have been egocentric issues on our two sons, already numb from a shift in the status quo.

I am drawn to resolution; am I able to step aside from my ego and serve? I have asked the question of myself and of others and I do believe I am.

The Alternative Dispute Resolution (ADR) course and mediation accreditation I earned gave me the finest faculty with which to begin. I found the course fascinating and truly challenging.

An earlier two-week period as juror was a vital experience, where life was about to be impacted permanently by a handful of us.

Following this, I represented myself in the Crown Court for my deceased mother. The judge was empathetic and listening intently to me. I was grateful; I asked to interrupt and he welcomed it. I came away with even more respect for those able to listen, with an array of valuable skills, amid the tides of conflict. I learned so much from the experience. Now, the courts are directed to support mediation and offer the service to all, in an attempt to bypass what can be a damning personal expense in all manner of heart, mind and bank account.

I was recommended to pursue ADR by a solicitor and a barrister, who thought I had the ability to discern with empathy. It is a humanitarian quest. I know this is a position of tremendous value in understanding the complex people we are and can sometimes become so witnessing the relief through the seeking of alignment and ultimately a settlement is a powerful driver.

Chapter Twenty-Seven
A Daughter's Turn

In 2011, my mother moved into a small, beautiful flat we had created for her within our home. It had its own front door and peephole; that message indicated privacy on all sides and was quietly harnessed. She loved it in her private space with our two boys there for bear hugs and two springers up for a walk at a moment's notice. I bought her a red walker from America. It had to be red, her favourite colour; it was built for uneven terrain, such as our paddocks and fields. There were horses in livery with us and their owners chatted with her when they were there and, most importantly, she felt safe within the privacy and the boundaries of the land. The beauty of the red walker was that if she felt her muscles twitch, it was time to open the walker and sit on its broad seat, grab her flask of coffee and read her newspaper. She would sit in the sun and snooze with the dogs at her feet. She also had a bell, in case of crisis, that could be heard for miles. I remember being at home with her every day, waking her with a coffee and a chat and tucking her into bed every evening. I was unable to leave her for more than an hour or two for over three years.

The doctor checked in and insisted on finding her a care home. He said, with gravitas, "Your Ma could fall, become distressed, need help with bathing and all manner of things." He was concerned that I had been virtually housebound for over three years and detected, before I had, that I was getting a little low. He said, "Christel, I'm getting that through the ether."

My mother adored him. Dear Dr Jonty is charming and very handsome; he always replied to her request to adopt him that he was a mummy's boy, so the answer was no – so sweet. There was always laughter.

There was a beautiful care home a moment's drive from my cousin Lotta's home; she was a dear friend of my mother and is trusted and close to me. Lotta's father is my grandfather's brother. Lotta visited my mother for coffee each morning and I visited every day, until bedtime mostly.

For me, it was an hour and a half's drive daily, but driving through Kent's back roads into luscious Sussex was nourishing and I didn't mind at all. My mother was happy and, honestly, all that mattered was that she felt safe. In the beginning, she found the care home to be a "hollow and benign place", but she tempered and enjoyed the bustle and the presence of others in earshot, adapting easily within a short period of time.

The staff did love her; her mind was clear, she was so bright, fun, and upbeat. She had her landline, forsook the telly, telling me she had watched sufficient episodes of *Murder She Wrote* and Agatha Christie's and 'Who Dunnits'.

Initially, there had been a two-week respite trial, so that I could go on a business trip to Toronto. I hadn't been able to leave her for more than an hour and a half, so when the doctor suggested his concerns, this was a way of testing the water. It took a little adjustment, but afterwards, she did reflect that she felt safe and secure with sweet carers and nurses, tending to her attentively – she felt safe in the palm of their hands.

One day, everything changed – it was like spinning on a sixpence! She fell and was found on the floor, sometime after calling out, not finding her alarm around her neck. Medical friends deduced that it was either a stroke that caused the fall, or a stroke as a result of the fall – who knew.

For a week she was hoisted with a broken spine – it beggars belief – sitting in nappies that tore at her dignity, in terrific pain but afraid, so she said nothing at all.

I asked for the diagnosis and I asked if I may be permitted to have a second opinion. The doctor in charge said, "Nothing wrong with her. Do as you want but there will be no ambulance – can't justify that. I'll leave the form in the surgery for you to collect." I was driving from Canterbury and met my cousin and sister at Pembury Hospital. Both agreed there was something unusual about my mother's face.

I had requested an X-ray. She had been squeezed into a car, in obliterating pain, screaming to get to the hospital. I asked the radiologist, post X-ray, "If it were your mother, what would you do please? He said, "I would take her straight to Majors, to the orthopaedic surgeon, and that is where I shall wheel her to, right now!"

After the diagnosis of a broken spine and a CT scan revealing two strokes, I telephoned the doctor's surgery and asked for my message to be relayed to the doctor who had misdiagnosed her. Suffice it to say, there was no response, except that on the following day, that doctor retired from her profession.

I took it to tribunal with support from adult social care because, as I left the hospital that night, I bumped into two carers from her care home, who were waiting to hear the outcome of a family member's crisis. Both begged me to report the misdiagnosis, since this was the fourth time it had occurred and, of course, those grieving know that arguing the point is deeply stressful and doesn't bring the loved one back.

Well, what a trigger that was for me!

A friend, who is a judge, said, "Where there is an injustice, I am a fearsome foe." In that moment, I understood. It was two a.m., I was in the car park, and *BOOM* – I heard the judge's voice resonating in my ear.

Three tribunal meetings were held in the care home.

Present were three members of adult social care, a nurse and the MD of the care home. Minutes were sent to the doctor who deigned not to attend. At the final meeting, I was asked what I wished as the final outcome. It was that the care home amended their regulatory instructions to permit the family's right to a second opinion after diagnosis. My request was granted. It felt just.

The episode was then formally closed. I was overwhelmed and emotional, feeling there would now be some level of justice for others facing such unspeakable heartbreak in the future. The episode was closed in hope and with reconciliation.

I fear those who knew her will be aghast to read this. Perhaps her illness might have subsided, as illness often can, if she had shared her fears. Perhaps the release of our fears can dissipate the onset, even vanquish disease? Perhaps gaining greater understanding of how powerful our emotions are can be an obstacle to illness.

The scientist Dr Joe Dispenza has a superb book entitled *You Are the Placebo* – it documents the vanquishing of symptoms and disease through the guidance of meditation. I have begun to learn so much from Dr Joe's work, he is one of my key mentors.

He has another book titled, *Becoming Supernatural*. In it, he writes:

'In 1991, the pioneering work of J Andrew Armour, MD PhD, showed that the heart literally has a mind of its own. With as many as 40,000 neurons, the heart has a nervous system that functions independently of the brain. The technical term coined for this system is the "intrinsic cardiac nervous system", more commonly known as the "heart brain". This discovery was so monumental that it led to a new field of science called neuro-cardiology. This evidence shows that Armour's discovery of the afferent, neural pathways from the heart to the brain proves that the heart independently processes emotions, responds directly to the environment and regulates its rhythms, without receiving information from the brain. That's because the ANS (autonomic nervous system) and the heart always work together. Simply put, our emotions and feelings originating in the heart play an important role in the way we think, process information, feel and understand the world and our place in it.'

In the end my mother did reconcile that my father always loved her, that his actions were borne of many things, not least a sometimes overbearing and overly strict schooling. I asked my father why he found telling the truth such a challenge. He told me he had been hooded at school for some childish misdemeanour and whipped with a belt. He couldn't and never did punish a soul, such was the impact of the disempowerment he had been exposed to. One human disempowering the other; add that to the list of discipline from his adored father, who was hardest on him as the eldest son of five children, and there you have it: a young man, with overwhelming compassion, attempting to bury a burden of unexpressed hurt. I began to understand the misuse of power, narcissism and more hideous human characteristics. I was truly relieved that the release happened with my father and later with my mother because I witnessed separately so much of their fear evaporate and I was able to genuinely hold them and give them both my understanding as a daughter, share their tears and affirm to them that their burdens were justified but gone now.

I'm mindful of this quote…

'And when I came in with tears in my eyes, you always knew whether I needed you to hold me or just let me be. I don't know how you knew, but you did and you made it easier for me.' – Nicholas Sparks, *The Notebook*

All I prayed was that taking me into their confidence, the speaking of it, would lift their burden, so it would feel easier, even if it had taken almost a lifetime. Maybe no one had ever asked them, maybe no one had ever wondered how they shaped their lives and why. God only knows that, if it were possible, I loved them more than before in that moment, with even greater respect for the adversities each had faced and turned into humanity, each in their own way; each on their own path.

Chapter Twenty-Eight
Evidence of Disease Profiles and Paradigms

Interestingly, on talking with her specialist, the most senior in the Southeast of England for elderly Parkinson's care, I asked if there was a profile for that illness. The great man was also a lay Baptist minister and, more importantly, he wore highly polished brogues, something my mother admired hugely – she had taught me that, "Your shoes reveal more of you than you'll ever know."

The specialist knew it all! He would firmly attest to my mother and he would always believe me first, he called me 'the bodyguard'. That was a relief, since every ailment she had seemed to dissipate and her most delightful and unproblematic side would emerge whenever she was in his company. Honestly, I could never fathom or contain my wonder at this. There's the sweet placebo that nestles in us, close to the surface, when we pull ourselves out of our mire – I got it.

She couldn't be a burden for this busy man that she had so much respect for. She was uplifted and felt safe in his presence. He became her favourite trip out and he was gentle and knowing with her.

My mother was like the phoenix born again through the flames when she saw him. We only ever saw this great man, we were never delegated to one of his team, he sensed absolutely that my mother felt grateful to be under his wing, that it mattered to her, that she felt safe in his judgement and care. He confirmed that Parkinson's patients have tendency to be controlling. They also have a 'pre-morbid speech' added to that; they seem to carry a looming bitterness just beneath the surface. The sad penalty of Parkinson's disease is the diminishing control over their bodies, rendering them almost helpless and reliant upon others, sharing every minute and all manner of mundane tasks – a constant reminder of their pathetic needs and awareness of the burgeoning anger from frustration, rising within them, needing constant assuaging whenever they are heading for 'melt down'.

My mother would plead, plaintively, "Where on earth does it come from, why does my body disobey, what causes this appalling weakness, what is it?"

Her sister had it also and somewhere, she watched a programme that alluded to the fact that Parkinson's was a virus stemming from Scandinavia! I don't know, although more recent research shows a link to the gut and the brain. I have learned every time we revert to a memory, we are propelled back into the place, into the same energy and somehow, we revert magically, mostly negatively, back into that moment. It's taken me years to learn how to put an obstacle between me and that process, so that when it triggers, I quickly remember I'm not in that life anymore, or even that person anymore. Goodness only knows the process can be the 'elephant in the room', but it is still a rewarding task to realise that part of life has ended and that, focused positively on change, we can choose to move forward.

I have met those who have been abused tragically, those who at a hundred paces can recognise damaging and abusive traits and yet, despite this, engage with the abuser, despite understanding the consequences – this is their base of communication. This is heart-breaking is it not? They say they are comfortable keeping the enemy closer – but those words, by the brilliant Chinese military strategist Sun Tzu, are there by way of intention to protect us by staying alert to the actions of our opponent.

'Hence to fight & conquer in all your battles is not supreme excellence, supreme excellence consists in breaking the enemy's resistance without fighting.' –
Sun Tzu

Apparently, this doesn't often work, since it can be all they truly feel familiar around, so they continue to receive and, on some level, consent to more abuse, sometimes for the rest of their lives. We must 'want' to change. It's difficult when our past dictates who we are and who we have become as our experience may dictate, but it's worth a try, and with support it can be accomplished.

During my first real heartbreak, I walked past a mirror in the hall of my flat in London and, in my peripheral vision, I saw this strained, wan face. I recall gasping audibly at my reflection in the mirror. I looked at myself and thought, no one should be able to 'do' anything to you at all, get a grip and stop it! I had to take responsibility for my own decisions. I understood that then.

Chapter Twenty-Nine
Life's 'Coaches'

One of the reasons for shying away from the title of 'coach' in my work and using instead accredited mediator, moderator, change agent or client relationship specialist, is that the title 'coach' has never been more popular. My frustration is fuelled by listening to the majority of 'coaches' one meets, who are not living their own strategies or creating an independent client. Rather than sharing their skills to empower their clients' independence, they are encouraging dependence.

There are top courses for an accreditation as a life coach and both my sons have been highly trained in this endeavour and I have full respect for that, but it seems the term has now become a generic term for a person with humanity. The responsibility demands more than that, it demands an education in the subject and accreditations are out there to be studied, approved and won. I am aware this may read as a sweeping statement and that there are superbly skilled and qualified coaches, and some close to me, who do empower and support, but the term 'coach' is, in my humble opinion, overused. I have been told that terms like mediator, moderator, change agent and so on are all life coach terms and apposite, but of course there are different levels, areas, systems trained for and employed, for each one.

Coaches working within the MSI businesses of network marketing in particular need to have a parental touch – not so in mediation. Mediation demands empathy not bias, concern not care, where listening without reaction, rather response to comprehension, are key factors for progress. All these components encourage autonomy, self-reliance and personal responsibility.

Chapter Thirty
Unconscious vs Conscious Parenting

It's possible that my mother guarded my brother rather too closely. There wasn't much room in that capsule for daddy and son adventures, they were virtually non-existent, any suggestion was avoided, yet conversely punished for its absence. Anyway, in the longer term, only two people suffered: the father and the son. It was a regret of my father's and one that created a ravine between them. My mother could often be found in the way, either by a subliminal need for allegiance from my brother, following my parents' parting, or by recounting stories of my father, borne of her sense of injustice, with a dollop of artistic licence as the icing – so, it could be said, it was complicated.

In hindsight however, babying my brother was self-centred, with every encouragement for him to lean on her and for him to reciprocate the gesture. It happens. I understand it. Conscious parenting can create a fine and trusting relationship with one's child by promoting independence rather than dependence.

My father's relationship with my brother may have been easier had his own parenting set the example. My grandfather was somewhat dictatorial, quick to use the whip, or his belt, when he felt his son's had misbehaved. It was brutal, a measure forbidden many years hence. Since, I have heard that my great grandfather employed the same corporal punishment on my grandfather and his siblings. My father didn't hold it against his father. Once he took my grandfather's car without asking and was whipped on his return. He took the blow and never held it against his father; it was forgotten and he strove to make his father proud for many years after his death. It made him sad that he and his own son struggled to find a common bond.

My brother was angry over my parents' divorce, my father lathered with the blame. This is an all too relatable outcome for children going through the dynamics of their family fracturing. With my own divorce, I promised I would forever be above critique of their father, at ease and fair.

I have a relationship view, as a parent of twin sons. We learn to parent as we go along but to have a relationship with either just out of mere duty rather than love makes me shudder and feels disappointing. If I can't listen to my children in a fixed position of support, if I can't adhere to that premise, providing safety and guidance, what kind of parent am I?

If I cannot set them free confidently onto the rollercoaster that is this world, by controlling and therefore stealing their unique experiences, what kind of parent am I?

I utterly adore my sons' company, together and on a one-to-one basis. Every moment and every effort has been a 'win', regardless of the ever looming exhaustion I felt when they were infants that came with submitting first to them, with myself last in line, because it is a privileged task to be the assistant, called on to wake and prep a young person for this life.

The love I have for our sons is complete. It is also 'sensible', with concern above all for their emotional and physical safety. It is also made up of awe and deep respect for these loyal, balanced, moral young men. Both have travelled alongside me without punishment of either of us, effecting discord in their favour, which might have been reasonable during the changing dynamics within the family. Instead, they brought their friends home, and our extended family has grown.

I have acquired a third son. His mother died too young. Her middle son has grown up with my boys, they have been best friends. He is ours and we are his. I must say we would all feel less without him in our lives, he has always been welcome and remains my third boy; we are devoted to him unequivocally. I have huge respect for his life and the patterns that emerge in him and us all as we traverse our experiences. I have urged him to remember he is ours and belongs; that is the only boundary.

I stood by, alongside, as much as is permissible as he floated through a phase of intense grief. I prayed that he would not feel that there was no use in the loss of his mother. I know he endlessly travelled with work to find refuge, needing and seeking solitude. I wished for him to feel at ease in us, his extended family. He is afforded the same licence of privacy and respect.

I understand mourning creates changes in us and like a kaleidoscope it may ebb and flow forever. Our mothers, both Ben's and mine, died in our arms.

We all need to feel safe in company and in silence. We all need to feel acceptable in any way, to be enough just as we are, as we stand. There is safety in being loved, and in the same vein feeling loved is what we all seek. I married a man I recognised would be the father of my children and was married for twenty-four years. We rub along well. I know him as intricately and intrinsically as he knows me. It was a good innings of a marriage. Today, one of the boys asked whom I trust in my life – he is one. My sons find this unique, but it also makes life so much easier for them. I tell their father often that I cannot do this without him; he is as important as I am and there is unity. We communicate for the love, stability, fun and privilege of being parents of these amazing young men.

I do not collaborate in disharmony, however many dalliances it took from yacht to shipwreck – that would be missing the point of my duties as a parent; his too, he agrees. The relationship with our sons now supersedes any relationship we may have had or may ever have. I am concerned for his well-being, as he is mine. He is a valuable, committed and loving parent and I couldn't do it without him. He has adoring and devoted sons who exchange with him daily – that for me is mission accomplished.

Chapter Thirty-One
Sabotaged – Triggers As Anchors

What is sabotage? It is the discreditation of another, of their strengths or gifts, the way they progress and express, often down to small details deliberately targeted to disable and undermine the other. It is borne of jealousy and of weakness towards what they see as some sort of power in another that threatens them. It is borne of fear and lack of self-esteem and, sadly, it is often those closest to us who do this. It is a trigger.

Like the wheelbarrow tipping up all the dirt that dumped itself on me, my sister's lack of any semblance of kindness was one such trigger. It was a betrayal – whatever the aim, perhaps there was none, but it served to momentarily stun and certainly I felt not a smidgeon of compassion from her for my situation. It lives on in my memory, and whilst I feel no bitterness, to the bewilderment of those closest to me, this is another important reason for the book.

My mother opened up to me, revealing why she had been hardest on me during my growing up. It was because she felt I had gifts or a tenacity that my sister and brother didn't possess; both were driven and motivated differently, which is quite normal. None of us are the same. I had an ability to lose myself in a hobby and lock myself away in my bedroom for hours on end singing, writing music, drawing. She said that every time I achieved a goal I had set myself she thought that made the others feel diminished. She felt that was my fault. I don't believe that for a moment and certainly don't recall any argument from my siblings at all – they were busy doing their own thing. It had become so silly and upsetting that when I cut my hair to a short bob, my mother exclaimed that I had made her day! I was in my forties! I had been the one with thick long hair, but goodness me – I was stunned.

Sitting with her there in the hospital almost twenty years later, I was humbled by the acknowledgement and apology from her even though it made me truly sad to listen to it – that all through my growing up, I was told to hide my light 'under a bushel' as she had called it. She felt I was highlighting that the others were not engaged in such hobbies and that meant they were somehow disadvantaged, which was never true; both my siblings excelled in those things they were drawn to.

It was sad that at eighty-five years of age she unburdened those things. I struggled not to well up; I'd buried those things, I thought, very deftly.

She told me she punished herself for not being beautiful enough for her husband, for not being enough to maintain her marriage, for being the second daughter, for the fact that people coming to the house thought she was merely the maid. In the end, she admitted she felt she was the driver in her own undoing.

Many moons after her divorce, three hundred and twenty-four moons to be exact (twelve moons or so a year, for twenty-seven years), we were sitting sipping chilled rosé in the garden. I asked her to consider forgiving my father since he had been dead for eight years – her reaction was to just blow a raspberry! I laughed and jokingly called her a baby. I said I felt she would sleep better that night if she could be compassionate with herself and learn how to forgive. Bless her, she was listening so intently. She faltered. "You really believe that?" I said of course I did, it had worked for me.

I asked her without any expectations, that if she could forgive, what would she want from it? She said she wanted to be free from always remembering the sad bits. She wanted to know if that would even be possible.

She called me early the following morning saying she felt happier than she had in a long time. She said she had made a commitment to forgive. I said, "You're a hell of a woman!" She laughed and said, "You know… I think I am!"

In his eulogy, her son-in-law, my former husband, spoke of that forgiveness and its almost magical dissipation of the heartache that haunted both my parents, my father because he had forfeited her and his family and my mother because she had forfeited him. Now the prize for that courage that released them both was peace.

Chapter Thirty-Two
'Do or Die' – The Hyperbolic Expressive

Should someone else's path destroy who we are, dismantling our innate joie de vivre? How tiresome that would be, not just for me, but for everyone and anyone close to that destruction, feeling they were in a tangled web of misery. Negative responses to our experiences, and how we react to them within, accelerate the growth of disease and there is more than substantial evidence to support this.

We will uncover more of the subconscious mind and its dependence and accountability for our actions later. Personally, I did not wish to become some hideous, dreary old witch wincing and bleating about men. It is a matter of choice, a decision I made, and I was staring at it squarely in my own reflection.

I must say, I have never disclosed these details to anyone, but I can only be honest and authentic in sharing my story. I hope that in admitting my frailty and my journey beyond, to survival, there may be a smidgeon of encouragement, a little nurture for another who may be inspired to stop for a moment to consider and begin to believe that there is a way through what seem like treacherous waters.

Perhaps someone will begin to create a new life, as I have done, and stop engaging with those miserable bedfellows such as bitterness, who nag to become your best friend. My heart feels the pain for you too. Shock has its destabilising impact. I know we can emit all sorts of sounds in a state of shock; hyperventilating is one of those and is quite normal. I think it punctuates a gasp of incredulity. It is involuntary and comes from an irrepressible part of the soul. I was stuck in this 'did I see this coming and what should I do now?' mode. It was a collapsing of that woman, the one who was once me.

Chapter Thirty-Three
Don't Look Back

Life is generous to me. I do make a point of remembering to live in gratitude. I believe that is the secret. Gratitude expresses faith. So, it is to abide in the ultimate state of receivership – a wish fulfilled, so to speak.

> *'Ask and it shall be given.'* – Matthew 7, 78

The latest scientific research proves the neural pathways in our brains can absolutely re-frame and alter our lives, create new genes and reorganise our DNA. Dr Joe Dispenza has clearly defined this in his work. His books *You Are the Placebo, Becoming Supernatural, Evolve Your Brain* and *Breaking the Habit of Being Yourself* are transformational; they offer the opportunity to gain a greater understanding into the actions we can take to adapt to a new way of thinking, in turn preserving our health and lengthening our lives, with purpose.

Dr Joe is a respected scientist, who thwarted medical advice to encase his spine to support the thoracic weight of his body when, at twenty-three years of age, he was crushed in a cycling accident and driven into by a car going at 55 mph that didn't stop! He went through what he called, "The dark night of the soul." Alone, he meditated, continually thanking God in advance for his ability to walk and continue his life's purpose. He used visualisation to see his spine healed and a mere twelve weeks later, he was walking unassisted, tending to his chiropractic patients. The event called true meaning into his life and determined his path. His meditations are powerful beyond measure and much research has been completed with ground-breaking and life changing results.

I have a gratitude list in my head. I can add more to the ten things I am thankful for each morning on waking and each evening on sleeping. The concept is so straightforward and these repeated thoughts tweak my perspective and steer the manner in which I manage my day. There are always unsettling moments in our lives, like those I share here. I don't regularly and actively wish to recall them, since I am not going in that direction. I am most determined that I am only going forwards.

It is noteworthy that what we think is, to a greater or lesser degree, something we choose to manifest in our lives. I have never been in therapy. I have leaned on one or two of my most trusted friends and my sons, in extremis, but I have never formally been to therapy. I do know it can be a rebirthing of personal validation and help to reinforce one's understanding of drive and purpose. I have many gifted colleagues qualified in this field, including both my sons and my sister-in-law, who play a key part in offering a strategy for their clients to re-establish purpose, empowering them to full independence.

Goodness knows it takes courage to reach out!

Goodness knows it takes courage to get there!

I hold an unwavering respect for those reaching out; for those born fine-tuned and trained in the attributes needed for this service. Seeing them help their clients through what tumultuous waters of heartache and pain they may be experiencing and assisting change by walking alongside them in step, affirming their courage as they begin to re-engage with this new path after trauma, is inspiring to witness.

For those brave enough to ask, who reach out, the support is always there. I always urge any friends going through the slightest wobble not to be alone. When we are out of kilter, it is important to reach out! This simple suggestion interrupts loneliness and depression (as so many of us hate to ask for help) and it can save a life. I know people who could not have continued a day longer without this support, who were experiencing indescribable depths of morbidity bearing down upon them. Jeopardy felt so close; it was as if they were losing control and heading downcast into a chasm. I have huge respect for the drive of purpose and support.

We are now experiencing a threat of global desolation and are suddenly humbled by those who serve on the frontline, whose quest it is to protect and save us and ultimately annihilate these mutating viruses currently in our midst. These people, who choose to submit to help as many as they can, are driven by something more powerful than is awakened in the majority of us… in it flows again, Agape love.

Agape love gives, not because of duty, but simply because it can. Agape is a gift. We can try to give ourselves the same gift; this includes the commitment to let go when we find ourselves in situations that do not serve us. It can be empowering and enlightening when we are challenged, to see how our heart and mind can be revolutionised, ready to begin again when we make the decision to let go of our heartache since it hurts only ourselves. There are plenty of ways to learn how to do this. Commitment is key and that is supported by self-belief and self-image. I have learned that release is a top goal.

Setting boundaries is pretty vital. I wasn't naturally good at these, which is one of the reasons I wish to impart them here. My father taught me to find what he referred to as 'a mitigating circumstance' for the person in dispute with me. He taught me so well that I became a little too good at turning the other cheek.

We all know that no one gets away with anything in this life, but still, we must apply our own boundaries and by that I simply mean we must remember that our self-respect is just as important as the other person's need for understanding, especially when they lash out or mismanage their treatment of us.

There is no excuse for venting onto another. If you are being vented upon, it is paramount for you to adhere to self-respect first. If you are on the receiving end of sabotage of any kind, just choose self-concern. We must decide and use our boundaries to support our emotional well-being and balanced survival. Let us attempt to vanquish the fear we feel beside or within us, that rallies to knock us off our feet; let us be bold when that old enemy rears its ugly head.

Chapter Thirty-Four
Earliest Instructions

The paradigms that shape us can be difficult to rebuff.

My father's father had his challenges as the youngest; when he was very young, he suffered from polio and wore special shoes to conceal that one leg was shorter than the other. He felt vulnerable with his disability. In adulthood, he became highly successful in the family's business, which cast us as a family across the world. Perhaps this adversity, this handicap, pushed him through with determination to be a success rather than be seen as a weakling. Scandinavia's part of the international business was co-created by his father (my great grandfather) and the originators, the Americans in Dayton Ohio, USA. It was the reason my father brought us to England in 1962, to work with the company here. The family sold up later in 1968, back to the US division.

My great grandfather had a legacy mentality. One of

the rules of the greater Holst-Sande clan that lives on today was that he, Johan Emmanuel, wanted each generation to know one another – to be committed to communicating with one another, always putting the family first. This directive still stands. We are all bound and happier for it. Whenever a family member arrives on your soil, wherever that may be in the world, the resident family 'stand', or as we say in Swedish 'staller upp', welcoming in the visiting 'rellies' as guests. It is huge fun and so interesting.

The women are nicknamed the 'Sande Women': strong, sassy and classic – big on living long and all that goes with that. Unafraid to remarry, they have seemed to re-educate at a later age and continue to stay teachable, always trying something new. The women are certainly not to be messed with! I always laugh when I hear the expression 'Sande Woman', but somehow it rings true looking at all the women in the family coins: that idiom 'cherchez la femme'. One example is of course the matriarch Wilhelmine Holst-Sande who passed away at one hundred and eleven years and eighty-nine days of age. With the strength of belonging in common, it's exciting to see the newer generations connect.

One of my sons was visiting America with two friends. Here were three six-foot-tall, strapping young men and still I suggested he give me his route so I could check in and know he was safe and recommend family members he could stay with along the way. Not surprisingly, he agreed and gave me their ideal and chosen route. I had so much fun planning and talking to my cousins. They hired a car and headed to Livermore first to a dear friend, whose son had been his bestie at school. Caroline Cambra, my lovely buddy, took them to hire a car, on my Costco account.

As a parent, I felt content to delegate to Caroline and to cousins in Sausalito, San Francisco and further. They visited Sonoma Valley for wine tasting, they stayed on my cousin Annika's Horse Ranch, had a musical evening there (we are quite a musical lot, undoubtedly borne of all those dark Scandi nights) with more cousins, before heading to Lake Tahoe to visit my bestie cousin Ellen and on, to San Diego.

The whole way round, my family opened their arms and welcomed in not one, but three young men and entertained them on boats and at wine tastings and had long, cosy chats into the night. I felt so blessed for this. We are well over six, nearing seven, hundred; we have a family group online and we cherish our heritage and our connections to one another.

Chapter Thirty-Five
Lessons From My Grandparents

My grandfather, 'Farfar', was king of his household and a sometimes stern parent. The rest of the time he would sing from the top of his voice, learn a new language, pontificate during his usual delivery of long speeches over every lunch and ponder life's meaning. He would trail, forever loved-up like a puppy, after his beloved 'Ta' (Märta), my grandmother. He loved his music and dinner parties and made life sweet for his grandchildren.

I asked her how she managed his endless devotion. My grandmother would say, "For the hottest, the love is the coolest. Never smother with your love, when one day you give your heart."

I believe those are Socrates' words:

'The hottest love has the coldest end.'

Apropos the advice from my grandmother on

managing each relationship, rather than relinquishing it to almost immediate disaster because our needs may blind us to our lover's needs, I wondered whether one might liken it to the most brilliant of stars, that bright light that when overwhelmed becomes an explosion.

This is a fair and important point. When we burn too brightly, we focus too intently on our own needs, on what makes us happy and thereby blindly become so intoxicated that we may neglect the desires and needs of our partner.

My grandmother, Anna Märta (the Contessa Af Verchou as she was), was spectacularly beautiful, part of a very early aristocratic family from Mecklenburg, Germany, naturalised as Swedes in 1664.

Their coat of arms is listed as number seventy-six since the inception of coats of arms. They are also listed in The House of Nobility in Sweden, 'Adelskalender' (the Swedish Directory of Nobility's Peerage).

My 'Farmor' (father's mother) embodied such humility and love and fun when we were small.

My grandpa, Farfar Arne, listened to the *World Service* long after dark but at a ridiculous decibel level. One night whilst staying with them in their home in Guadalmina, Spain, around midnight, hearing the rather loud radio, I caught the dulcet tones of Julio Iglesias. I got up from my bed. There was my Farmor, sashaying in her beautiful nightdress as always, hugging a cushion to her, dancing to Julio Iglesias.

It was so loud, it drowned out the booming *World*

Service.

My grandparents had moved to Spain from Sweden for some sunshine. My grandfather was called 'the man with the instant garden', with avocado and lemon trees that naturally flourished in the sun.

I recall lots of Fanta Limon and Naranja bottles in the cupboard, for smaller people like me. He had exquisite taste and was a spectacular host. I spent many holidays there alone with my grandparents; it was a privilege. Once, he took me to a picador bull fight. I recall feeling bewildered by it and switched off in shock. We left. It was a mistake. I was too young, too affected. I found it so unforgiving; I was heartbroken.

We went to a shop and I chose some colouring felt tip pens and special art paper. I soon forgot my tears as he sang, "Blue skies smiling at me, nothing but blue skies do I see…" Oh! He could sing. I was enchanted and comforted all the way home; he was harsh, but he was also a dear heart. He also took me to the village fiesta in San Pedro, where he held my hand so firmly as I gazed, enchanted, at the Spanish boys who called me 'Guapa' and liked my blonde hair. In an attempt to stop them following me, he growled, rather loudly, "Basta!" ('Enough!') – I remember it so well; it was so funny!

I did adore my time there. He taught me backgammon. He would sing loudly when I was pondering my next move, deliberately competitive; it was of course done to put me off. He would look at me out of the corner of his eye to check whether his deliberate interruption was working and then he would burst out laughing. He had a compelling twinkle in his eye; he would swing his legs like a child whilst sitting on the end of the diving board over the pool, in his own world. He expressed his love easily to me – I have been so lucky.

Their Swedish home, 'Fullersta Gård', in Huddinge, was host to magnificent banquets and, on one occasion, I was seated, awestruck, next to the very handsome French singer Sacha Distel. I was twelve.

At another memorable celebration, 'Oldemor', my great grandmother's ninetieth birthday party, I wore a kilt and danced The Highland Fling, which I learned at my ballet classes in England. My uncles and father all played behind me on double bass, clarinet and piano. I was given a 'slant', a few pennies from my great grandmother for dancing.

Sweet memories. I remember we all sang *What Will We Do with a Drunken Sailor*, but I don't think we sang all the verses – having looked them up today!

That evening, at the end of the party, the extraordinary Wilhelmine, my great grandmother, flew unaccompanied to New York and on to Tucson to visit one of her daughters, Tulla. She visited America eighty times in total during her lifetime.

I was present at Wilhelmine's 110th birthday celebrations. It was a huge drinks party with family in Stockholm. Though we were all family, some of us met there for the first time, which I recall felt so exciting.

After the drinks, her remaining five children and twenty-three grandchildren went for dinner. My great grandmother contributed thoughts to the speech that evening, although she didn't attend, of course. According to my mother, her oldest son Uncle Johan (Johnny) relayed that she had said she had been born on the sunny side of the lake (translation – jag va född på solsidan av sjön).

Wilhelmine was worshipped by all; the king and queen of Sweden visited her each year after her century for tea and 'torta' cake! On her death, the Crown's flag flew at half-mast over Stockholm, where she lived out the last few years of her life. The greatest longevity of a woman in the Nordic countries at that time, though this has maybe been superseded by now.

Fullersta Gård in Huddinge, which is now an art museum, is full of memories of the raspberry canes and the 'boccia bana', the boules lane that my Farfar loved so much. He also imported English roses for the centre of the drive around the flagpole and had a cellar full of delicious wines beneath the entrance at the front of the house. He was a workaholic, gregarious, strict but playful. I remember he challenged a friend to paint something and cheated – he thought no one would ever know; he traced the painting and proceeded from there – I don't recall the outcome, but it amused him hugely. My grandmother and aunts also had séances at Oldemor's home – the glass moved (honestly) of its own accord! We called in a ghost called Esther. She had previously been a maid (not sure exactly when) and had fallen in love; it wasn't reciprocated. She hung herself in the ceramic stove and her spirit never left. I never could sleep in my great grandparent's home Stensättra after that!

Chapter Thirty-Six
A Privilege to Walk the Whole Way to the Gate

My mother, Eva Margareta Lindahl Holst-Sande, died in my arms at 4:09 a.m. on 18th October 2016. I wrote this to my siblings and her inner circle:

Good morning,
 Mamma 'slept in', as we say in Swedish, at 9 minutes past 4 this morning.
 I was holding her gently as I recited our favourite childhood prayers, 'Gud Som Haver Barnen kär'. I sang 'Sov Du Lilla VideUng' most quietly, her favourite nursery rhyme. I told her of God's Heaven, as much as I could imagine it, of the music and his Angels, of the sunshine and the ease with which she would now be able to move her limbs; of God's strength, and his welcoming of her into his home with rescue and love.
 She is lying next to me and altogether in another

world and yet already I want to wake her. I ache physically from missing her. She was so calm and so dignified. I listened to her heart beating – the nurse told me not to be afraid and to listen through the stethoscope.

It sounded like the water lapping against the wooden rowing boat on the lake, reminding me of every Nordic child's experience of lying in a tethered boat, with the cluck-cluck of the water against the hull.

Her favourite nurse, Christina, woke me at 3 a.m. saying we had an hour left of her lifetime. I had slept alongside her for 6 days and nights.

As I held her in my arms, I prayed so hard for God to help her to forget all that hurt her in this life and to reassure her that each step forward would bring her soul only sunshine, that she would recall nothing but love.

Now, it seems empty already. It is the finest privilege to have walked with her the whole way to the gate, to God's door.

My mother's eyes were closed for the last five days. On the final day, I asked her if she wished to be alone, since I had been told that was what many leaving this life wished for. I had heard of friends who had left to fetch a cup of coffee and returned to their loved one and found they had departed during their absence.

My mother objected to my question by grasping my hands so tightly – I said of course I would be with her every moment, and only then did she release her grip. She could still hear me until the very end and just before she died, she raised her head a little and opened her eyes and looked straight at me. It was unexpected and absolutely stunning!

From the moment my brother heard of our mother's death on that morning, he yelled that he "detested" me – she had not waited for him to arrive from Paris before she died, perhaps this may have triggered his wrath. He detested me because I would not prohibit Ma's friends or her spectacular and much-loved carers, whom she adored and who adored her back, from attending her funeral. Forgetting that the funeral was about his mother, he refused to attend, but his children refused to miss it.

I couldn't find it in my heart to prevent my mother's friends from attending. It felt like madness; cruel, self-centred. When she died, the carers with whom she had made such precious friendships cried over her body without restraint and said their prayers out loud for her. It was such a shock to us all, so sudden. I could never have disallowed them or my mother's best friends of more than fifty years of friendship from attending her funeral as my siblings demanded.

When I asked my sister why she made such a decision not to permit this, she replied that she didn't want people to see her cry. The response from the vicar was simple astonishment, since the day was about her mother and no one else. Our vicar, who adored my mother, affirmed the church was closed to no one, certainly never to those in mourning.

I was resolute at that moment that I had to stop this misery driving its way through my family during this period of high emotion and heartache. We were thirty-six guests at the funeral. My gallant, former husband stood between my siblings and me; he was my strength and protection for which I am forever grateful. He also wrote and read the eulogy, visited the church with me, did all the prep alongside me, took charge over the wake whilst I, stunned and floating, was apparently somewhere floundering, far away and dazed.

My parents' six grandchildren stayed with me the night before the funeral. I did not interrupt their evening, save to prep their beds, their supper and lay and light a roaring fire. I stayed in the kitchen, so they would not be chastised by their parents if I joined them. They popped in and out of the kitchen; we all shed our tears and had hugs together. My former husband had given me champagne for my birthday, as he always does, and those bottles were enjoyed by the grandchildren – one each. They had huge fun together and they are my parents' legacy.

The cousins live apart, two in Paris and, at that time, one at St. Andrews University with the other three in London. They have so much fun together, getting on so well. I am happy for that. I'm proud that they chose to be together the night before a very big moment in their lives, their grandmother's 'Goodbye'. Quite rightly, they felt life too precious to give credence to any trials their parents might have been facing.

My siblings' visits to my mother were rare – to my father, there were no visits at all and there have been none to his grave. Indeed, it is a sad fact that the elderly in care homes are rarely visited by their family – this is one of the greatest sadness's I witnessed; it broke my heart.

My mother's mind was sharp as a blade even at the end; little eluded her, she was a no nonsense 'Tenko', a vibrant character. I treasured her company.

I have never lived alone with only my memories as my companion. I have never lived alone with frightening thoughts of what might become of me. At the end, she'd always ask, "Christel, what will become of me?". It was a lingering fear. After a lifetime of doing her level best for everyone else, she found herself bereft and without purpose. It was purgatory – a waiting room, where she went over and over her life, longing to put certain things right, certain conversations straight. She longed to give comfort where she felt she had been too self-centred to reach out.

She wanted to ask for forgiveness for moments where she spoke hurtfully without a care and a thought. She wanted to say sorry and hold the child she punished as an overly strict parent. She did have that opportunity to apologise to me for punishing me for the independence I expressed and the passion with which I followed my dreams, as she had. She said it made her think my siblings would feel inadequate but she also knew it was she who felt she had left her dreams behind. I was a constant reminder of how it was to be young and carefree, without entrapment of family; however much we were loved, she felt she came a long way down on the list as the mother.

She knew why she was angry.

She longed for compassion and understanding; she was only a child in the end, having never truly vanquished her fear of inadequacy that began when she was small. For an independent woman, to be utterly dependant is not a path of repose. If I could lift her spirits just by being with her, focusing on her, asking her questions of her life, I would do so every day. It was a mark of my love and respect. It is also a measure of how I was brought up, even if that duty wasn't shared equally.

We are all on our own paths and make our own decisions. I cannot judge, even if sometimes now I am incredulous over their lack of focused commitment to their parents – after all, we came from the same nest.

Chapter Thirty-Seven
Lemon-Lipped Women

I never wanted to join the 'Men Loathers' or the 'Divorced Women's Club' – obviously not!

Becoming a wizened, lemon-lipped woman because of an inability to let go and forgive would spell disaster.

Everyone in the world now knows how stress races through every vessel and steps up to disease. Science and medicine support this. I shall keep recommending books that explain easily why cortisol is an enemy to be thwarted; it is scientifically proven as a gateway to 'interference with learning and memory, lowering immune function and bone density, adding inflammation that leads to weight gain, high blood pressure, cholesterol and then heart disease... the list goes on!' (Christopher Bergland, *Psychology Today*, January 2013).

Am I afraid to love again? No, of course not...

Well, a bit.

I want to occasionally feel enveloped in a strong-minded and faithful man's arms; someone who likes me and what is important to me, someone who openly cares, as I care, mirroring the affection, the fun and the interest. That is my wish, but isn't that everyone's wish, to meet on the bridge in an equal partnership.

I happen to adore men; I like the differences between us. I learned to love men a long time ago. I enjoy my girlfriends' company, but so many of them spend their lives talking to their girl buddies about their men and their foibles rather than communicating with their partners, who say they would honestly prefer us to be clear, since they say they are appalling mind readers.

My darling father, whom I felt most comfortable around and whose love and concern for me was the clearest formulae I was exposed to as a child and as a young woman, was able to read and access my inner fears. He knew as a young woman I had no idea of the impact I had on the opposite sex and so, like most fathers, he was protective of me and set on teaching me to be safe – he did this as a formality and part of his responsibility as my father.

He adored my former husband and most every boyfriend I ever had, because he could see they loved me and were genuinely good chaps and they made me smile. When he died, his son-in-law wrote a sensitive and beautiful eulogy, expressing his sadness at losing a dear friend.

Chapter Thirty-Eight
Save Our Souls

I recall the drawing room at the time. It still had the same ancient and worn curtains left behind by the former family. They had been deliberately kept during years of postings abroad with the army. Kept by way of providing a constant. They were pale blue – a pretty cornflower blue – plain but, as luck would have it, they (almost) fit the windows. The room was pretty, with candles lit, a fire laid and flourishing. The warmth of the setting had been prepared for 'The Talk'. What had also been prepped was the overnight bag.

The planning had clearly been done earlier; bag popped in the car, ready for the smooth exodus, the sort of action that feels like a disappointing 'skulking' around the place. I was at the time bathing two small people, about to hit their third birthday. Of course, they consumed most of my waking moments; they occupied my mind, body and soul. They were my soul where my sanity resided and still does. To this day they remain the finest privilege and fill us both with unfettered joy.

The fire was laid and supper made, the wine breathed to the perfect temperature. And so, The Talk began.

I sank into a heap. I might still be there, but I had responsibilities. I had to hold the fort. Bear my burden. I had two babies and had to carry on.

He… well, he was having a crisis and wanted me to see him as the victim.

'Victim stancing' is a power behaviour that exploits the desire of others, to help someone who is in distress. It is also based on an external focus of responsibility. It denies choices that do exist. It turns the non-agreement of others into an injury.'

People may all too harshly criticise the stance of the victim, as the definition above illustrates. Of course, there is always responsibility for whatever scenario we find ourselves in but just sometimes, there are greater factors to consider – one such factor drives this book. That evening, his alibi faltered. A teeny mistake was to ask one of his oldest, lifelong friends, godfather to one of our boys, to provide his alibi. I was upset. I rang the friend without reply. The friend didn't wish to court conflict and felt it wrong to be drawn in and didn't wish to be disrespectful of me. It made me consider the part of the alibi. I felt, then and now, that one must find courage and, whatever the circumstance, stand in the truth.

There is always an impact and a reaction; a beginning

and an end; a negative and a positive; light and dark. It's another of the Universal Laws, the Law of Compensation, which in simple terms states that we are always compensated by our actions.

In his *Essays: First Series*, Ralph Waldo Emerson wrote, 'polarity, or action and reaction, meet at every part of nature; in darkness and light; in heat and cold; in the ebb and flow of waters; in male and female; in the inspiration and expiration of plants and animals; in the equation of quantity and quality in the fluids of the animals; in the systole and diastole of the heart; in the undulations of fluids and of sound; in the centrifugal and centripetal gravity; in electricity, galvanism and chemical affinity. The same dualism underlies the nature and condition of man. Every excess causes a defect and every defect an excess. Every sweet hath its sour; every evil its good. Every faculty which is a receiver of pleasure has an equal penalty put on its abuse. It is to answer for its moderation with its life. For every grain of wit there is a grain of folly. For everything you have missed, you have gained something else, and for everything you gain, you lose something. If riches increase, they are increased that use them. If the gatherer gathers too much, nature takes out of the man what she puts into his chest; swells the estate but kills the owner. Nature hates monopolies and exceptions. The waves of the sea do not more speedily seek a level from their loftiest tossing than the varieties of condition tend to equalize themselves. There is always some levelling circumstance that puts down the overbearing, the strong, the rich, the fortunate.'

We must know this then with certainty, that we receive what we put out and that there is nowhere to run.

I received a book from my son when he was twelve, with the parallel sayings of Jesus and Buddha. I found it expanded my thinking. This example is from the book *Jesus and Buddha – The Parallel Sayings*.

'Many false prophets will arise and lead many astray and, because of the increase of lawlessness, the love of many will grow cold.' – Matthew, 24, 11-12

'Monks who are untrained will give guidance to others and they will not be able to lead them in the way of higher virtue. Those in turn who have not been trained will give guidance to others and will not be able to lead them.' – Anguttara Nikaya, 5, 79

Christians are taught that 'sin is not ended by multiplying words, but the prudent hold their tongue.'

Buddhists speak of 'right speech, abstentions from lying, divisive speech, from abusive speech and from idle chatter.'

Hindus state: 'if a man be his own guard, let him guard himself against rage. Left unguarded, his own wrath will annihilate him.'

Islam says: 'most of the quarrels arise out of evil and irresponsible talk and the major sins that are commonly committed are also related to the tongue.'

Those are just four of an apparent four thousand three hundred religions in the world giving firm advice to their believers.

Spirit fathoms all things, it is omnipotent and omnipresent, waiting until the dawning of all the consequences of our actions. One has to face up squarely to one's reflection in the mirror. Our reflection may feel distorted when we are destabilized. If we do not own up, recoiling at the demolition that we are party to, our spirit is roused, recoiled. Running from ourselves just confines us and becomes a prison. Our Spirit nudges us to wake up.

The mind and body sit alongside, dovetailing, abiding together. Like the vascular system, one stream connecting all, so every part of us bears the impact.

The soul is, I believe, who we are, in our purest essence, our better or best nature. God and goodness reside in our soul with the spirit, never apart, always in tune, never separated. It's the part that saves our sanity; it is us, the finest part of us.

Epilogue

I began to discern the vulnerable from the strong when I was very young. How to deflect a comment too uncomfortable to address, how to find a way of managing every day has been, for me, a valuable tool. We are only human after all. If it matters at all, we long to be understood, particularly under duress, and we fight for that right.

As an accredited mediator I have learned so much by way of listening, without bias and prejudice to those in dispute. I am happy that now mediation is offered to all and can pave the way for resolution. I am interested and pleased that mediation is being taught in schools – it is quite different from the classes where we engaged in when I was young. We are a diverse culture with a melting pot of thoughts, traditions and heartfelt reason for living by the rules that are the essence of our families, some that travel back through centuries. The understanding and respect we need to extend to another, be it our child or partner, our work colleagues or friends, even when there is an understandable divide by way of culture, is vital. Hopefully, now in these times, we are beginning to reach out when things are tough and addressing those parts with well-being and resolution as our goal. This compassion must start in our families.

This permission to speak without judgement, gives room for reason, even if it is drop by drop, deliberately seeking to avoid the injury of pride. It can give us all an opportunity to walk away from dispute and begin life again, agreeing to differ, but without shame. I have always valued the great military strategist Sun Tzu.

Sun Tzu, ancient Chinese Military General, in as early as the 5th century BC said this:

'If you know the enemy, you know yourself, you need not fear the result of a hundred battles. If you know yourself but not the enemy, for every victory gained you will also suffer a defeat. If you know neither the enemy nor yourself, you will succumb in every battle.'

My instinct says people do not need to be 'told'. We all think we have a good measure of most of the stuff going on around us. I enjoy connecting with someone's personal experience that has moved them. Perhaps they, like me, have been moulded and finely re-tuned into a whole new human being.

I am sure we do benefit from our adversities.

I know I empathise more easily and have a greater conscious humility that has crept in as a result of my challenges. Empathy must surely be the best way to communicate.

The people I admire have a few attributes in common. They are calm with sophisticated listening capabilities, they are built of persistence, courage and faith. They are excited by this glorious, yet imperfect world we live in. They create their own paths, responding rather than reacting to outside influences, which usually head with speed to nowhere at all.

I do believe that if we are really awake and listening, disasters and horrors may perhaps not befall us. If we look after our mental health and those dependent upon us, with peace as our weapon, life has a real chance of serving us well in return.

These words have been written from a stronghold of peace. Peace is always the preferred weapon in any misunderstanding – none of this was ever going to be easy. These words of mine come from a place of gratitude; gratitude for the harmony that has waged a war against opinion and finally paved a way of freedom for us all. Change rocks foundations. Ours were built on footholds of true concern and love for the family we created and for all those we love.

Undoubtedly conflicts disturb and stir deep rooted memories that we, as individuals, bring to the leap of faith that is suspended over every marriage. Clearly, we are not responsible for every burden we carry, we inherit much from our parents – mostly doing their level best. Once acknowledged, however, as adults we should ask ourselves whether we seek the courage to do things our way, without asserting the blame elsewhere or holding others accountable, so that we have the chance to stand in our truth, responsive and not reactive.

We can choose to honour the commitments to our family and to those demands placed upon us all.

If we are supporting change with empathy and integrity, tricky as it first may seem, we do have the chance to nourish our lives going forward.

Hopefully you may see this book as an affirmation of the importance of meeting in the middle, agreeing to disagree, walking forward without shame, with integrity clasped firmly in both your hands.

Family and our children are the finest privilege after all.

In taking positive action there is hope for everyone's future and, dare I say it, our mental health.

Every blessing and betrayal is vital in shaping who we become and how we serve and love others. Every mistake is an obstacle removed from our path, making way for something greater.

I recall the boy whose Ford sat in the drive of his grandmother's home. He repeatedly told her, "Granny, one day soon, I'm going to have a Lamborghini." She always smiled and replied, "There's a Ford in the driveway, there's no space for the Lamborghini!" – one day he finally understood the metaphor!

The message here is, let the vehicle that took you through your past be replaced with something you aspire to achieve, whatever that may be. Make space for it! As long as it's not another 'Ford' – the past – you have heeded the lessons and demanded something different that serves your health and happiness and future better.

I wish you the drive of your life!

With love and my blessings for your future adventure,

Christel